PREACHERS I HAVE HEARD

Dr. ALEXANDER WHYTE

*Reproduction in colour by Edward Drummond Young, Edinburgh
from the portrait by the late Sir James Guthrie
Inserted by kind permission of Sir Frederick Whyte*

PREACHERS
I HAVE
HEARD

ALEXANDER GAMMIE

LONDON
PICKERING & INGLIS LTD.

Pickering & Inglis Ltd.

29 Ludgate Hill, London, E.C.4
229 Bothwell Street, Glasgow, C.2
59 Cross Street, Manchester, 2
105 Bold Street, Liverpool, 1
95 St. Mary Street, Cardiff
56 Grainger Street, Newcastle upon Tyne
29 George IV Bridge, Edinburgh, 1
Home Evangel, 418 Church Street, Toronto, 2

First published - - *1945*
Reprinted - - - *1946*

Made and Printed in Great Britain

PREFACE

WHEN it was first suggested to me, and I agreed to act on the suggestion, that I should put in writing my recollections and impressions of preachers I had heard during a fairly long experience, I had no idea of the extent to which the project would grow, or of the very wide area that would be covered. But I had been in the way of hearing preachers, national and local alike, whatever their doctrinal beliefs or their denominational allegiance, and when I wrote of them my concern was primarily with their preaching.

This seemed to appeal to many who were interested in preachers beyond as well as within their own particular schools of thought. From readers, both at home and across the sea, came letters of appreciation, followed later by repeated requests for the collection and re-publication of the articles. It is in response to these requests that this volume is now being issued.

As the articles first appeared on the Church Page of the Glasgow *Evening Citizen*, I am indebted to the editor of that paper for permission to re-publish them. My thanks are also due to the owners of photographs and the photographers who have given valuable assistance in completing the gallery of portraits. Of a few preachers of the past it has not been possible to secure photographs from which such perfect reproduction could be made as in the case of the others, but not one is missing.

It would have been invidious to make a selection from living preachers: hence their omission. Articles called forth by special circumstances have been left in their original form, but the date of publication given will sufficiently explain contemporary allusions.

ALEXANDER GAMMIE

To
MY WIFE

To
MY WIFE

CONTENTS

CHAPTER   PAGE

   I Dr. Alexander Whyte 11

  II Dr. George Matheson 14

 III Professor David Smith 19

 IV Dr. James Macgregor 24

  V Principal A. M. Fairbairn   27

 VI Rev. John McNeill 31

 VII J. G. Paton and James Chalmers .. 35

VIII Dr. Joseph Parker 39

 IX Professor James Stalker 42

  X Laws of Livingstonia 46

 XI Dr. John Hunter 50

 XII General Booth 53

XIII Principal John Cairns 57

 XIV Dr. J. H. Jowett 60

 XV Principal James Morison 64

 XVI Rev. C. Silvester Horne   68

 XVII Dr. T. De Witt Talmage   71

XVIII Rev. W. J. Dawson 75

 XIX Dr. George Macdonald   79

 XX Rev. Hugh Price Hughes   82

 XXI Dr. Ambrose Shepherd 85

 XXII Professor James Moffatt 89

XXIII Ralph Connor 92

XXIV Dr. Alexander Smellie 95

 XXV Rev. Donald McIntosh 98

XXVI Dr. Donald Fraser 101

XXVII Dr. Walter C. Smith 104

XXVIII Dr. John Ker 107

XXIX Professor Robert Morton   110

 XXX Dr. James Hastings   113

XXXI Dr. R. F. Horton 116

CHAPTER		PAGE
XXXII	Rev. A. E. WHITHAM	119
XXXIII	Dr. ALEXANDER GRIEVE	122
XXXIV	Dr. JOHN KELMAN	124
XXXV	Dr. D. M. McINTYRE	128
XXXVI	Professor W. P. PATERSON	131
XXXVII	Dr. F. B. MEYER	134
XXXVIII	Rev. G. A. STUDDERT KENNEDY	137
XXXIX	Rev. WILLIAM STODDART	140
XL	Dr. MARCUS DODS	142
XLI	Dr. DINSDALE T. YOUNG	145
XLII	Professor H. R. MACKINTOSH	148
XLIII	Pastor D. J. FINDLAY	151
XLIV	Dr. ARCHIBALD FLEMING	155
XLV	Rev. GEORGE GLADSTONE	158
XLVI	Principal JAMES DENNEY	161
XLVII	Rev. J. P. STRUTHERS	164
XLVIII	Dr. J. D. JONES	167
XLIX	Rev. T. N. TATTERSALL	170
L	Rev. W. H. LAX	173
LI	Dr. JOHN WATSON	176
LII	Dr. G. H. MORRISON	179
LIII	Principal W. M. MACGREGOR	182
LIV	Dr. F. L. WISEMAN	185
LV	ARCHBISHOP TEMPLE	188
LVI	Dr. GEORGE JACKSON	192
LVII	Dr. G. CAMPBELL MORGAN	196

ILLUSTRATIONS

WHYTE, Dr. ALEXANDER   ..   *Frontispiece*

FACING PAGE

BOOTH, GENERAL   56
CAIRNS, Principal JOHN   48
CHALMERS, JAMES   32
CONNOR, RALPH   81
DAWSON, Rev. W. J.   64
DENNEY, Principal JAMES   157
DODS, Dr. MARCUS   148
FAIRBAIRN, Principal A. M.   17
FINDLAY, Pastor D. J.   149
FLEMING, Dr. ARCHIBALD   156
FRASER, Dr. DONALD   96
GLADSTONE, Rev. GEORGE   156
GRIEVE, Dr. ALEXANDER   117
HASTINGS, Dr. JAMES   116
HORNE, Rev. C. SILVESTER   49
HORTON, Dr. R. F.   116
HUGHES, Rev. HUGH PRICE   65
HUNTER, Dr. JOHN   48
JACKSON, Dr. GEORGE   193
JONES, Dr. J. D.   176
JOWETT, Dr. J. H.   60
KELMAN, Dr. JOHN   124
KENNEDY, Rev. G. A. STUDDERT   125
KER, Dr. JOHN   97
LAWS, Dr. ROBERT   33
LAX, Rev. W. H.   177
MACDONALD, Dr. GEORGE   65
MACGREGOR, Dr. JAMES   24
MACGREGOR, Principal W. M.   192

9

McINTOSH, Rev. DONALD 96
McINTYRE, Dr. D. M. 124
MACKINTOSH, Professor H. R. 149
McNEILL, Rev. JOHN 17
MATHESON, Dr. GEORGE 16
MEYER, Dr. F. B. 125
MOFFATT, Professor JAMES 80
MORGAN, Dr. G. CAMPBELL 198
MORISON, Principal JAMES 49
MORRISON, Dr. G. H. 192
MORTON, Professor ROBERT 112
PARKER, Dr. JOSEPH 40
PATON, J. G. 32
PATERSON, Professor W. P. 132
SHEPHERD, Dr. AMBROSE 80
SMELLIE, Dr. ALEXANDER 81
SMITH, Professor DAVID 16
SMITH, Dr. WALTER C. 97
STALKER, Professor JAMES 33
STODDART, Rev. WILLIAM 148
STRUTHERS, Rev. J. P. 157
TALMAGE, Dr. T. DE WITT 64
TATTERSALL, Rev. T. N. 176
TEMPLE, ARCHBISHOP 188
WATSON, Dr. JOHN 177
WHITHAM, Rev. A. E. 117
WISEMAN, Dr. F. L. 193
YOUNG, Dr. DINSDALE T. 144

I

Dr. ALEXANDER WHYTE

THERE has been no preacher in living memory of greater personality, preaching power, and abiding influence than Dr. Alexander Whyte, of St. George's, Edinburgh.

So much has been written about him that it is almost impossible to say anything new. But in my gallery of "Preachers I Have Heard" he could never be omitted, and I have at any rate some personal recollections of one of whom it has so often been said, "He was the last of the Puritans."

From time to time I received letters from him written in his own characteristic style. On New Year's Day, two years before his death, he described himself as "an infirm old man far from home, and for the most part of my time in bed."

Then he went on to say: "I spent last Sabbath on a book that I read for the first time more than fifty years ago. It is the work of an author who has never been out of my hands for all these many years. And as I read that book again the thought was again and again in my mind that I will now set down for you to pass on.

"Let any of your Divinity student readers early discover and select some great author or authors in divinity; let those great authors be to them all their days something like what Athanasius was to Newman, and Augustine to French, and Luther to Bunyan, and Leighton to Coleridge, and Butler to Gladstone, and Foster and Faber to Marcus Dods, and Hooker and Bunyan and Butler and Law and Goodwin to myself. And, sir, I do not know that I could send student readers, or indeed any class of readers, a better New Year advice along with the best benedictions of an old and ever-grateful student."

The last communication I had from Dr. Whyte was written from Hampstead not long before his death. It was a pencilled post card—he rivalled Gladstone in the use of post cards—and the writing was more shaky than ever.

After thanking me for some article I had written—nothing escaped him, and he was always ready with a word of appreciation and encouragement—he concluded, according to a habit of his, with some lines then running in his mind:

> *Let not conscience make you linger,*
> *Nor of fitness fondly dream;*
> *All the fitness Christ requireth*
> *Is to feel your need of Him.*

Even his appearance in the pulpit was arresting and impressive. "Look at him," it has been said. "The frame has a lean squareness suggesting muscular power, the hands are almost fleshless, with a bony grip on the sides of the desk, the face has a singular straitness and severity and pale light in it. High straight brow, large hollow eye-sockets, long lines of spare cheek and thin mouth crossing each other, a square chin; all are marked, all convey their hints with startling decision. The eyes lift but seldom, the close lips hardly open, yet after a sentence has passed they set at the corners with finality."

He was at his best when he was preaching and aflame with passion. Then the whole man became transfigured. He was once described as a thunderstorm, "a two-legged whirlwind," as Kingsley said of Synesius.

Emphasis has always been laid, and rightly so, on what has been called Dr. Whyte's "acute and often morbid anatomy of sin." Once Dr. Whyte and Ralph Connor were walking in the Pass of Killiecrankie and talking of Henry Drummond. Suddenly Whyte stopped and said with a twinkle in his eye, "The trouble with Hen-a-ry is that he doesna ken onything aboot sin." He himself seemed to revel in revealing the sinfulness of the human heart—his own most of all. The criticism was heard that he was too introspective, too morbid, but it was his deep sense of sin that gave to his preaching of the grace of God a passion and power it might not otherwise have possessed.

As prominent in his preaching was his power to rise on the wings of his sanctified imagination. For long years he carried out his own precept—"Let your imagination sweep up through the whole visible heavens, up to the heaven of heavens. Let her sweep and soar on her shining wing, up past sun, moon, and stars."

A young man in Edinburgh who came under the spell of Whyte's preaching writes: "Vividly dramatic at times, he makes you see things that are invisible. In a truly terrific passage he was picturing 'the hunting hounds of sin' on the trail of the sinner. 'Hearken!' he cried, lifting his eyes from his manuscript and gazing into the corner behind me. 'Do you not hear? See! Yon long, lank, lean-bellied hound making up on ye.' For the life of me I could not forbear a quick glance over my shoulder. Great preaching! With a swift change of tone and manner he pictured the sinner's escape into the 'warm, strong, loving arms of the Heavenly Father'."

Like other famous preachers—and others less famous—Dr. Whyte had his special sermons. One of them was on the Ransom, which, on the testimony of many witnesses, was an unforgettable event in the spiritual life of those who heard it. Sir William Robertson Nicoll, who was present in St. George's, wrote at the time of the "rare wealth of imagination and emotion" which was poured into that discourse. Scarcely less moving was the prolonged soliloquy of the sermon, "I Was Crucified with Christ," or the imaginative power of that on "The New Wine of the Kingdom."

Of Dr. Whyte on the platform, I have one very vivid memory. It was at a great public meeting on the occasion of the jubilee of the '59 Revival. There was a congenial atmosphere, and he revelled in his subject. His address was delightful in its reminiscences, and some of the thumb-nail sketches he gave of prominent figures in the movement were inimitable in their pawky humour and their lifelike portraiture.

What could have been more graphic than his picture of "the North Pole and the South Pole, both discovered long ago, when a stately Presbyterian divine, one of the most handsome and best-groomed men in the country, preached in the open air alongside the 'Briggate Butcher' of Glasgow, who had a face that might have been hewn with his own meat-axe, minus an eye, which he lost in one of the fights of his unregenerate days, and a voice like a bull of Bashan?"

His address, so human in its touch, and surcharged with a depth of emotion and spiritual fervour, swept all before it. He seemed able to touch every chord—at one time stern and austere as a Puritan, at another beaming benevolently on his audience, and at still another with flashing eye and sweeping gesture rousing them to a pitch of enthusiasm.

Some one once said of Dr. Whyte that he was "always like a fire on a cold day." But nothing better was ever said of him than by his fellow-native of Thrums, J. M. Barrie, who wrote: "To know Dr. Whyte was to know what the Covenanters were like in their most splendid hours."

October 19, 1940

II

Dr. GEORGE MATHESON

DR. GEORGE MATHESON was born in Glasgow and, at the end of an eminent career spent elsewhere, he was buried in Glasgow. It was the city in which he received his University training; in which, as assistant to Dr. J. R. Macduff in Sandyford Church, he had his first experience of ministerial life; the city also around which clustered many of his fondest recollections. And Glasgow has reason to be proud of this son of hers whose name is so assured of enduring fame.

It is undoubtedly as a hymn writer that George Matheson is best known throughout the world. No hymn by a modern writer is more familiar or more frequently used than his "O Love that wilt not let me go." It was first published in the Church of Scotland magazine *Life and Work;* it was afterwards included in the Scottish Hymnal; and to-day it is found not only in the Church Hymnary of the Presbyterian Churches but in the hymn books of churches of all denominations in almost every land.

So many conflicting accounts have gained currency regarding the circumstances under which the hymn was written that it may be well to quote Matheson's own statement. He said: "My hymn was composed in the manse of Innellan on the evening of 6th June, 1882. I was at that time alone. It was the day of my sister's marriage, and the rest of the family were staying overnight in Glasgow. Something had happened to me which was known only to myself, and which caused me the most severe mental suffering. The hymn was the fruit of that suffering. It was the quickest bit of work I ever did in my life. I had the impression rather of having it dictated to me by some inward voice than of working it out myself. I am quite sure that the whole work was completed in five minutes, and equally sure that it never received at my hands any retouching or correction. The Hymnal Committee of the Church of Scotland desired the change of one word. I had written originally 'I climbed the rainbow in the rain.' They objected to the word 'climb,' and I put 'trace'."

It has been said that "whatever may be the future of his other writings, this hymn will be sung by congregations of the Christian

Church everywhere so long as the Cross and the Divine Love of which it is the symbol will continue to lift up the head of fallen humanity."

Matheson himself always regarded this hymn as his *piece de resistance*. But other hymns of his have found a place in many modern hymn books and are regularly used. One of them, which is included in the Revised Church Hymnary, is the beautiful

> *Make me a captive, Lord,*
> *And then I shall be free.*
> *Force me to render up my sword,*
> *And I shall conqueror be.*
> *I sink in life's alarms*
> *When by myself I stand;*
> *Imprison me within Thine arms,*
> *And strong shall be my hand.*

Another which is not so well known but has been included in the collections of some churches, although not in the Church Hymnary, is that which he entitled "One in Christ," and based it on Ephesians 1. 10: "That in the dispensation of the fulness of times He might gather together in one all things in Christ."

> *Gather us in, Thou Love, that fillest all!*
> *Gather our rival faiths within Thy fold*
> *Rend each man's temple veil and bid it fall,*
> *That we may know that Thou hast been of old;*
> *Gather us in!*

> *Each sees one colour of Thy rainbow light,*
> *Each looks upon one tint and calls it heaven;*
> *Thou art the fulness of our partial sight;*
> *We are not perfect till we find the seven;*
> *Gather us in!*

By his devotional works also Matheson gained a wide constituency. His " Moments on the Mount," "Searchings in the Silence," "Words by the Wayside," "Leaves for Quiet Hours," "Rests by the River," and other similar works, had a great circulation in his lifetime, and they are still read and treasured in many quarters. He was a practical mystic, and therein lay a large part of his popularity and influence as a devotional writer. Then he had a rare gift of style with a charm and a music which made an appeal at once artistic and spiritual.

In another vein he published numerous philosophical and religious works. Many consider that the finest book he ever wrote was his "Studies of the Portrait of Christ." Dr. Alexander

Whyte, one of his ardent admirers, wrote at the time, "It is a true test of a work of genius that its touch fertilizes the mind of the reader, and my mind and my heart have both been fertilized to-day over your deep and beautiful book."

Of the countless number of people who know and have been influenced by Matheson's hymns and devotional works comparatively few can claim any knowledge of him as a preacher. Yet he was one of the most powerful and appealing preachers of his day. In his ministries at Innellan and St. Bernard's, Edinburgh, he attracted overflowing congregations. No man of his generation had greater pulpit popularity. The blind poet-preacher was like a magnet to the crowds of learned and unlearned alike. His congregations, it was said, were drawn from all classes of society, clergymen, leading members of the Bar, University professors, scholars and scientists, artisans and workmen, and while he never despised those occupying good social positions, his democratic spirit seemed intensely gratified by the fact that the common people heard him gladly.

He had a real gift of oratory. His voice, as I remember it, was strong and powerful, at times somewhat harsh rather than melodious. But his fervour of delivery carried everything before it. And he had a rich sense of humour which often stood him in good stead, while his own zest in his subject was quite infectious.

One of the most brilliant students of his time at Glasgow University, Matheson had intellectual powers of such a high order that he seemed destined to be an apologist. Indeed, he himself thought that he might be able to do something in harmonizing the old faith with the new. But as time went on he abandoned this line of thought with which "his searching intellect and his deep heart had grappled, and turned his face to the spiritual East. He set himself to live more truly the life that is hid with Christ in God. . . . The dayspring from on high visited him more and more gloriously. . . . Even in the darkness of this world the kindly light was about his feet and on his face. He was strengthened to the end, and strengthened many by the ancient succours of the soul."

It was a liberating experience for Matheson when he left philosophies largely alone and concentrated on spiritual preaching with all his rare gifts of originality and imagination. It was not in Scotland alone that he was in demand for preaching engagements. England and Ireland also made demands upon him. One of his greatest appearances was made when he was the special

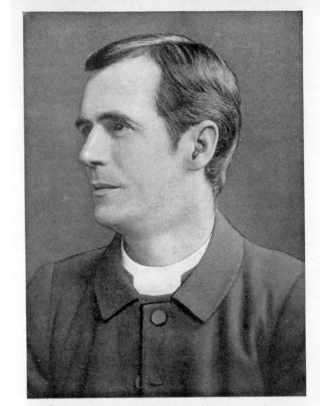

Professor
DAVID SMITH

Photo:
MARSHALL WANE & CO.,
Edinburgh

Dr.
GEORGE MATHESON

Photo:
HORSBURGH, Edinburgh

To face page 16

Rev.
JOHN McNEILL

Principal
A. M. FAIRBAIRN

From the portrait by Sir George Reid

preacher in Brunswick Chapel, Leeds, on the occasion of the annual service of the Wesleyan Methodist Missionary Society. The vast audience inspired him to one of his mightiest efforts.

As an instance of how he could rouse and thrill many different types of audiences, the story has been told of the occasion when he preached the annual sermon of the Primitive Methodist Conference. His text was: "Who are these that are arrayed in white robes?" He portrayed heaven as a vast concert hall, and asked his audience to take a sweeping glance over it. "Who are these in the centre, *before* the throne?" For answer he quoted part of the text—"These are they," etc. "Who are these, and these, and these?" He replied by mentioning different classes of Christians. Then he asked: "Who is that man at the very back of the hall, the man with the pale, thoughtful face? That is Spinoza. He has only got an angle of the truth, but he is working his way to the front, to the centre." And from all parts of the hall there came cries of "Hallelujah!" and "Help him, Lord; help him, Lord."

While he could stir such audiences to scenes of religious fervour, he was equally successful with those of another type. No preacher was more popular with theological students, and in University circles generally he was a great favourite.

It has been said that a sermon by George Matheson seized the hearer, would not let him go, and accompanied him through life. Ministers used to be almost afraid to read his sermons because of the danger some day of using not only the thoughts but the words. That was because of their freshness and originality and arresting power of expression. In Edinburgh his preaching was particularly helpful to two classes—students and other young people fighting with their intellectual and other difficulties, and doubters who were groping their way to something definite. But to all classes he had a message, and he never disappointed their expectations. "If," it was said, "the day was bright, he used the very sunshine to illustrate the Eternal Light; if the day was depressing, he used the gloom to illustrate the clouds and darkness of experience, on which he managed, somehow, to pour a radiance of Divine mercy."

At one time in his Edinburgh ministry it was suggested that he might relieve himself of part of the service and get his assistant to take the prayers. His reply to his well-meaning friends was both pointed and characteristic. "Prayer," he said, "never causes me an effort. When I pray I know I am addressing the Deity, but, when I preach, the devil may be among the congregation."

A well-known minister who recently retired from active

2

service, and as a young man was frequently drawn to St. Bernard's and profoundly influenced, writes: "Dr. Matheson's first prayer was often the finest part of the service. And what a prayer it was! A lifting up of the heart and upraising of the spirit, a reaching out after God, an outpouring of the soul, like the rapturous song of the lark, mounting higher and higher into the blue, to find in the limitless skies the satisfaction of its whole nature. I confess it was this first prayer that often lifted me up into the Mystic Presence more than any other part of the service. How difficult it was to keep the eyes closed! There, upon the high pulpit, was the blind poet, with uplifted hand, always reaching out and into his own illumined darkness, as if trying to catch something of the mystery of God and draw it down to man. He carried us all up into the heights along with him, and he drew down for the most commonplace of us something of the transfiguring blessing; so that, often before the rapture of aspiration was over, the eyes that watched the blind praying man in the pulpit had to view him through a mist of unconscious tears. Through this man's aspiration God laid His hand on the heart of all of us. In other churches we could get more sustained eloquence, more elaborate theology, more orthodox statements of Christian doctrine, but in this poet-preacher there was the illuminating flash of a Divine imagination which revealed the beauties of many a hidden truth; there was an aspiration and an inspiration and a spiritual glamour which created an atmosphere of worship that infected us all with a sense of God's very self."

Personally, I received from Dr. Matheson, in my early days as a writer, such encouragement as affected my whole life. I keep one of his letters among my most cherished possessions.

When he died it was said of him: "It is not the night but the light that has fallen on the strenuous brave life of Dr. George Matheson. He has received a house from heaven, where they who look out of windows are not darkened."

January 7, 1939

III

Professor DAVID SMITH

IN the death of Professor David Smith I have lost one of my oldest
and best friends. The news came on Sunday as a shock, for
his illness was very brief. He had been planning another book;
he had even told his doctors about it, and up to the last, as long as
he was able, he kept talking about it, and discussing how it was to
be done. But suddenly he passed away, and countless people in
all parts of the world—not least in Glasgow and the West of
Scotland, which he loved with an unchanging love—have been
plunged into mourning. The deepest sympathy goes out to his
two sisters, both of them in weak health, who are bowed with
mourning in their darkened home.

It is unnecessary to refer in detail to the facts of Dr. Smith's
career. These have already been given: my tribute to his memory
will be of a more personal and intimate nature. It is based on a
friendship with him and his family extending over a long period of
years, a friendship fostered by personal intercourse of the most
delightful and memorable kind, and maintained, even at a distance,
by a correspondence of rare interest and value. I treasure bundles
of Dr. Smith's letters, written in that wonderful printed script
which made every one of them a work of art. In these letters of
his are comments and criticisms which would shed many a
revealing light on the ecclesiastical and religious history of our
time.

While fragile physically, there was nothing weak about Dr.
Smith otherwise. The way in which he triumphed over his
infirmity was a proof of his pertinacity and of his possession of an
iron will. He overtook more work than many a strong man would
care to face. And while in his personality there was the gentleness
of a woman, there was also another side to it. He was courageous
and fearless to a degree. His convictions were not lightly held,
nor hidden under a bushel, and he was human enough to have
strong likes and dislikes. He had, when he cared, a power of
pungent speech, and he could call a spade a spade as well as any
one I ever knew.

It must be said that it was a lasting regret to many that Dr. Smith

was ever lost to Scotland and to his own Church. He had taken
his place in the front rank of New Testament scholars, and his
name was put forward for the New Testament Chair in one of
the Church Colleges in Scotland. He received very influential
support, and everything seemed to point to his election. It is
unnecessary to-day to raise the embers of an old controversy
which waxed fierce at the time regarding an ecclesiastical move
which was strongly denounced in some quarters as Machiavellian.
When Dr. Smith was passed over, an outcry arose which gave
him an unexpected public prominence.

Shortly thereafter he entered on a month's holiday pulpit
supply for a friend, and from the first Sunday the church was
crowded. The people flocked from all quarters, and finding they
had discovered a preacher, they went again and again. Dr. Smith
suddenly discovered his own pulpit power. All the quiet years
in the little church at Tulliallan had unconsciously been a preparation for this supreme opportunity. The eagerness of the people
to hear him, and their responsiveness to his preaching, called forth
his best, and he threw himself into it with a quiet intensity and
power of thrilling effect. Nor was this merely a passing phase.
Having once captured the ear of the public he retained it ever after,
and became one of the most popular preachers in the land. Wherever he went, in city or in country, he was followed by crowds.

There can be no doubt that the experience through which he
then passed, and which was so strongly resented by his friends, left
a scar which he felt intensely, and continued to feel for many a day.
But Scotland's loss was Ireland's gain, and he found great and ever-
increasing happiness as a Professor in the Irish Presbyterian Church,
to which he gave all the love of an adopted son.

Dr. Smith's name will live by reason of his published works,
and perhaps most surely by the first and last which came from his
pen: "The Days of His Flesh" and "The Disciples' Commentary of
the New Testament." The first was undertaken at the request of
the late Sir William Robertson Nicoll, that great discoverer of new
talent, and I quote Dr. Smith's own words to me in regard to an
interesting incident in connection with it. "It was," he said, "a
formidable undertaking for a novice in bookcraft, and I faced it
with much trepidation. Late on the day when I completed it I
was looking over it in my study, and so dissatisfied was I with my
work that I decided to burn it. I had stirred up the fire, and was
just about to consign it to the flames when my sister Jean entered
to bid me good night. On learning what I was after, she snatched

it from me, and despatched it next morning to the publishers in London." So nearly was there lost to the world a famous work which has gone into sixteen editions and has been translated into several foreign languages.

In his study Dr. Smith was surrounded by books on every hand. The collection of classical authors indicated the bent of his mind, and many fine editions of the Fathers adorned his shelves. Professor A. B. Bruce, whose teaching so largely influenced Dr. Smith, introduced him to his first charge at Tulliallan. Dr. Smith told me that, as they sat talking in his study after the day's work was over on that Sunday long ago, Bruce said to him: "You will find no inspiration in your surroundings in a country parish; seek it in your books." "And so," continued Dr. Smith, "I did. It was a continual wonder to me later on that in those early days, with a total income of £153, I continued to spend never less than £30 a year on the purchase of books—the great, enduring books which are 'a possession for ever', among them one year the Benedictine St. Augustine, at a cost of 12 guineas."

But something else was sure to attract the attention of a visitor to Dr. Smith's study. One, two, or even three cats might have been seen among Patristic folios, or perhaps perched on some eminence, from which one would unexpectedly descend on the visitor's shoulder as a convenient step towards the floor. Of his dogs he wrote time and again as his beloved companions, with whom he was on terms of an almost human understanding and sympathy.

Of Dr. Smith as a preacher much could be said. It was my privilege to hear him many times and in many places. Almost every sermon in his volume, " Man's Need of God," I have heard from his own lips. It is, however, difficult to convey to others an adequate impression of his peculiar power. It was unlike that of any other preacher I have known. He had none of the common arts of the pulpit—in voice, manner, or deportment. But from the moment he opened a service he seemed to have his hearers in thrall.

One of the secrets of his power was that he seemed to bring a spiritual atmosphere with him. Here, one felt, was a man who came forth from the inner place with its fragrance about him although he wist not that his face shone. No one could forget the radiant, gracious smile which often lighted up his features, or the voice, vibrant with emotion, as he spoke of "Our Blessed Lord"— a phrase often on his lips. His sermons were fine examples of the

homiletic art: they were intensely practical, for he dealt faithfully
with sin; but perhaps above all they were winsome and appealing.
He was at his best when extolling the love and grace and attraction
of his Saviour:

> For, ah! the Master is so fair,
> His smile so sweet to banished men,
> That they who meet Him unaware
> Can never turn to earth again.

One sermon of his—on "The Face of Jesus"—I can never forget.
Those who have only read it in booklet form can have no idea of
the impression it produced that night. There was a church
crowded to overflowing and a congregation listening in eager,
almost breathless, attention. The preacher was aglow with
adoration. I can still hear him saying, as he said more than once
that night, "What a Face that must have been!"

The manner in which he closed a service was deeply impressive.
His benediction was that "Peace be with us in our going out and
in our coming in, till we all come at last to our Father's house, to
go no more out for ever," and then, with his hand still upraised,
he pronounced the final words:

> O may we stand before the Lamb
> When earth and seas are fled,
> And hear the Judge pronounce our name,
> With blessings on our head.

While a scholar of the first rank and immersed in the study and
writing of theology, Dr. Smith made no parade of these things in
the pulpit. There were often illustrations, particularly fresh
and telling, drawn from his very wide reading in Patristic
literature, but many of the other illustrations he so freely used
were drawn from the simple scenes and common incidents of daily
life. These were told with a consummate literary skill which gave
a grandeur to the commonplace. Simplicity was one of the outstanding characteristics of his preaching, but it was the simplicity
which is the highest form of art. With his tender touch, he had
always a message of sympathy and help, a message born of his
personal experience, for those who had been bruised and broken
in the battle of life. Many will remember how David Smith's
whole being seemed almost transfigured when he spoke of Christ
and

> How He walked here, the shadow of Him Love,
> The speech of Him soft music, and His step
> A Benediction.

With all his gifts as scholar and mystic, theologian and preacher, Dr. Smith had no greater gift than that of his personality. In its winsomeness and graciousness, its tenderness and fragrance, it was a personality of no ordinary kind. No one was more delightfully human. Although it might not have been generally known, he had a rich vein of Scots humour. I have met few men—even few ministers—who had a greater love of a good story or could tell one to better effect when he was seated at the fireside with his pipe in his mouth. At the same time, it was in private intercourse one got to know how real and rich was the spirituality of the man. He was one of those who could talk to men face to face of the things of the soul as easily as in the pulpit, and without any suspicion of sanctimoniousness or affectation. When he spoke of spiritual things his voice became reverent and tender and his face glowed as with a hidden light.

Dr. Smith was the guide and counsellor of so many people all over the world in their difficulties of faith and conduct that his passing leaves a sad blank. But for him there need be no sorrow. "He was ever a student of divinity, and all that has happened is that he has gone to study where the divinity is clearer." Much of his time here was spent in communion and fellowship with the unseen, and he must find himself very much at home in the new life on which he has entered. "So he passed over, and all the trumpets sounded for him on the other side."

November 20, 1937

IV

Dr. JAMES MACGREGOR

THERE was no greater pulpit orator or more popular public personality in the Scotland of his day than Dr. James Macgregor. It was not in Edinburgh alone that he dominated the scene. He was known all over the country: stories of the man and his influence seemed to have permeated the national life.

It has been said that for many years Dr. Macgregor was "one of the tourist sights or 'sounds' of Edinburgh."

Great numbers of Americans were always to be found in St. Cuthbert's, and in his prayers he included a petition for the President and people of the United States, although one of them remarked with a twinkle, "But they tell me that he only puts up that prayer in the summer months."

That was one of Macgregor's little idiosyncrasies. Another was his innocent pride in having friendships among the great in the land. "We pray for the Duke of Argyll, who is worshipping with us to-day" would call attention to the presence of one who was among his most intimate friends but happened also to be a duke. On the other hand, however, "the doctor" was as much at the service of the humblest as of the highest; and up many a long tenement stair his little legs carried him on visits of help and consolation.

As a boy his physical deformity had been such that a neighbour asked his mother what was the use of educating one with such natural disadvantages. Her reply was brief and to the point: "Jamie has pairts." And her confidence was to be more than justified.

An occasion has been recalled by Dr. Lauchlan MacLean Watt when a Lecturer on Pastoral Theology had been insisting on a big, strong physical frame being essential for a minister. "Just then the door opened and he who was affectionately known as 'Wee Macgregor' entered as though in challenge of the statement. The house nearly came down with our applause. For that figure, with short twisted legs that dwarfed him, was the triumphant vindication of the transcendent independence of the spirit over the handicap of the body."

Even Macgregor himself had at first some doubts as to his

Dr. JAMES MACGREGOR

To face page 24

future. "Seeing myself such a poor little figure," he said, "I took
to learning Gaelic to fit myself for the only charge I thought from
my personal appearance I could expect to be called to, namely
that of a Highland parish."

But his fears were soon falsified. After a short assistantship at
Newton-on-Ayr, he was called to the High Kirk, Paisley, and
ordained to the ministry of that large and important congregation
in his twenty-third year. Before he left for the country parish of
Monimail seven years later, he had "packed the High Kirk from
floor to gallery." In less than two years he was back to a city
charge as minister of the Tron Church, Glasgow. There he soon
filled the empty pews till Norman Macleod, of the Barony, described the crowd as "A Macgregor Gathering."

When, in less than four years, he left the Tron in Glasgow for
the Tron in Edinburgh, he had to explain to Queen Victoria at
Balmoral, as best he could, the origin and meaning of the word
"Tron".

It was during Macgregor's ministry in the Tron Church in
Edinburgh that Dean Stanley went to hear him and formed a life-
long friendship. A.K.H.B. has told how Stanley afterwards said
of Macgregor: "Yes, he is a great orator. You can no more
judge what he is in a pulpit from seeing him waddling about
Westminster Abbey than you can judge of St. Paul from his epistles!"

Before six years had elapsed, Macgregor was called from the
Tron to St. Cuthbert's. In 18 years he had been in four charges,
but he now settled down to a ministry of nearly 40 years in one
place, and it was as " Macgregor of St. Cuthbert's" that he attained
his greatest fame.

In the pulpit of St. Cuthbert's Dr. Macgregor reigned like a
king on his throne. His popularity was not a passing phase; it
continued undiminished to the very end. As an orator he was
supreme. With his fire and fervour, his flashing eyes, and his
wonderful voice, which could reproduce every emotion, he
seemed to have all the endowments for oratorical effect. What
an extraordinary impression he could make with that voice! The
story is told of an occasion before the outbreak of the South African
War when he referred with intense feeling to "the unworthy letter
of the German Emperor to President Kruger." The words were
few and simple, but for those who heard them there was more
than the words: there was fire and magic and the whole passionate
soul of the man. "There was a movement," it was said, "a sound
of feet, and a low murmur of assent which brought an instant

sense to the preacher that he had roused the passions of men. With upheld hand and telling voice he bade them for God's sake to sit quiet, and in a moment he had them at peace. His was the magic of the orator, that indefinable quality which has ever swayed men as the winds which pass and are gone."

One occasion on which I felt all the thrill of his voice stands out in my memory. It was in the verse from Revelation: "And I heard as it were the voice of a great multitude, and as the voice of many waters, and as the voice of mighty thunderings, saying, Alleluia, for the Lord God Omnipotent reigneth." The crescendo in his voice grew until the concluding words, "The Lord God Omnipotent reigneth," came like a great shout of victory, ringing and triumphant. It would be as impossible to convey any idea of the effect as it will be ever to forget it.

Dr. Archibald Fleming, who was once his assistant, has spoken of how Macgregor's thunderous voice could become subdued to the note of a dove, and how the eyes that flashed in furious lightnings over the crowds became soft and caressing as a mother's.

Among the secrets of Macgregor's power as a preacher were his knowledge of human nature and his intense interest in men and women of all classes. They felt that he shared their own hopes and fears; and thus, it has been said, "he won his way to the very centre of their being—as poets and prophets have always won their way—by saying those simple and final things about the heart of man which men recognise to be universal and eternal."

But there was more than that. He had a very direct and affectionate and personal relation to Jesus Christ, and this completely coloured his preaching. He once declared with perfect truth: "All through, from the beginning, I have tried to be true to my colours—preaching Christ and Him crucified. The rock of my faith is the eternal Sonship of the Lord and Saviour, Jesus Christ."

And so his influence remains not by published sermons, for in cold print they could never convey the power of the man, but in lives which he touched to higher things. The memory will long be cherished of this little man of deformed physique, of amazing vitality and vivacity, and of irrepressible and often boisterous humour, who, with all his towering gifts, had the heart of a little child and never lost his simple childlike faith.

March 23, 1940

V

Principal A. M. FAIRBAIRN

I AM not dealing here either with the story of Principal Fairbairn's career or with his standing and influence as a theologian.
For the moment, I am concerned purely with his preaching. It
was as a preacher he first made his name, and he continued a
preacher to the end.

Although it was as Principal of Mansfield College, Oxford,
that Fairbairn rose to the height of his fame he never lost his Scots
characteristics. He lived the greater part of his life in England,
but Principal Denney truly said of him he could never be an Englishman. Nor, for that matter, did he ever want to be other than a
Scotsman. He loved the hills and dales and rivers of his native
land; all the sights and sounds were dear to him to his dying day.
One of the finest things I ever heard him do was when, in course of
a sermon, he declaimed Robert Louis Stevenson's lines:

> Blows the wind to-day, and the sun and the rain are flying—
> Blows the wind on the moors to-day and now,
> Where above the graves of the martyrs the whaups are crying,
> My heart remembers how!
>
> Grey recumbent tombs of the dead in desert places,
> Standing stones on the vacant wine-red moor,
> Hills of sheep and the howes of the silent vanished races,
> And winds, austere and pure.
>
> Be it granted me to behold you again in dying,
> Hills of home! and to hear again the call—
> Hear about the graves of the martyrs the peewees crying,
> And hear no more at all.

Neither before nor since have I heard these lines rendered as
they were by Fairbairn that day. Many years have passed, but I
can still see him in the pulpit, wrapt, absorbed, his voice vibrant,
and his whole being charged with emotion. He was so thrilled
himself that he communicated a thrill to his hearers which some of
them can never forget.

In the days when he was a minister in a charge of his own,
Fairbairn is said to have been seen at his best in his wonderful
Sunday morning services. Robertson Nicoll has written of them

thus: "There was a mere sprinkling of strangers in addition to the regular congregation. One was struck by the grave, subdued air of the worshippers. Most of them were evidently poor, though decently clad. Not a few had drunk the cup of sorrow. They had found life a 'sair fecht'. They needed consolation and strength. They turned to Fairbairn in the pulpit their weather-beaten faces, brows furrowed with care, eyes that had shed difficult tears, and had sometimes lightened with unearthly lustre. The most beautiful thing, as it appeared to me, in Fairbairn's character, was the way in which he set himself to succour, to uplift, to inspire the flock committed to his care. In my mind his morning sermons were far superior to his evening lectures. They were simple, but full of pity and sympathy. The preacher knew what his hearers were thinking and needing, and what they had experienced. His prayers, in particular, were very memorable, and a few sentences have lingered with me, like this one, 'Some of us live by the sweat of the brow, and some by the sweat of the brain, and some by the sweat of the heart, and that, O Lord, Thou knowest, is the hardest sweat of all'."

It was, however, by his sermons on special occasions that most of us knew Fairbairn as a preacher. Like his famous Sunday evening lectures, they were profound and lengthy treatises. It has been said that "at the end of forty minutes he would amaze his hearers by hinting that he was now nearing the suburbs of his central subject."

Dr. A. E. Garvie, in his autobiography, tells of an occasion when Fairbairn officiated for him on a special anniversary occasion in Montrose:

"On Sunday morning he preached a beautiful sermon on 'The Love of Christ constraineth us'; although it lasted fifty minutes it was much appreciated. In the evening his subject was, 'What think ye of Christ?' I recognised purple passages from lectures, and he discoursed for seventy minutes to the bewilderment of many hearers. When, in giving out the last hymn, he made a reference to the occasion and expressed regret that time had not allowed for an adequate treatment of his subject, an old woman forgot her manners, and exclaimed to her neighbour, 'Guid God, he's nae gaun to begin again!' "

Evidently Fairbairn appreciated the story, for he afterwards told it against himself in Oxford.

Fairbairn's gift of language was something phenomenal. He had come under the spell of both Macaulay and Carlyle, and his style has been well described as having in it "Macaulay's strings of antithesis and Carlyle's gnarled sententiousness." When once he fell into antithesis the sonorous rhythms rolled from his lips like a Hebrew chant.

Those sermons of his were on the grand scale. A critic once remarked that "he could 'splash at a ten-league canvas with brushes of comets' hair,' so opulent were his historical resources and so wide his horizons." His massive, thought-crammed, ornate discourses moved with a majestic sweep, but they were also hot with conviction and aglow with enthusiasm.

There is a story told of an old farmer who used to drive four miles every Sunday to hear Fairbairn preach during his first ministry in Bathgate, and was chaffed by his friends one market day at not being able to understand what he heard. But nothing could shake his faith in Fairbairn. His reply to the suggestion that he was unable to follow all his minister said was: " Maybe aye, and maybe no; but, man, it's grand to sit in front o' the laft and catch the sough o't gaun past yer lug."

It was a youthful hearer who wrote of Fairbairn's preaching: "Truth to tell, we could not always follow him. He went beyond, he dived beneath, he soared above all that we could reach or fathom or attain to. This I often felt, and sometimes, I remember, grey-bearded hearers made confession of it. But all the while we knew he was on the track of truth, and, if he was lost sight of now and then, we but watched for the returning swoop that brought his argument within our humbler ken. It was fell preaching and grand training for the younger hearers."

It may seem rather extraordinary, but it is none the less true, that Fairbairn as a preacher was specially popular with working people. One of his students explained it very aptly thus: "They like to hear Fairbairn because he is so sure, so earnest, so enthusiastic, and if they are unable to follow all his reasoning they go away none the less happy, encouraged by the thought that so earnest a man is a true believer. When a great man makes his boast in the Lord, the humble hear thereof and are glad."

He published a volume of his sermons under the title of "Christ in the Centuries." Some of them were strictly pastoral in tone and scope, and marked by depth of thought, fineness of feeling, and at times by real eloquence of expression. But very little idea of his power as a preacher can be gathered from the printed word. One had to hear them delivered with all his passion, and fervour, and abandon.

Fairbairn was a pulpit orator of the old school, a school practically extinct to-day, and it is something to be able to recall such a master of that school.   But there was a tremendous sincerity about him.   He always gave the impression that he was speaking, not by rote, but out of a knowledge and experience he had won for himself at a great cost like (to use one of his favourite passages)

> Iron dug from central gloom
> And heated hot with burning fears,
> And dipt in baths of hissing tears,
> And battered with the shock of doom
> To shape and use.

Rhetorical he certainly was, in a manner that was magnificent and moving in his day and generation, but behind all that, and along with it, he had a mighty intellectual sweep, an amazing erudition, and a grasp of theology that was as wide as it was profound.   Would that style of preaching make the impression to-day it did then? Who knows?   There is this to be said, that Fairbairn had, in addition to all else, some of the things that always make preaching worth while, whatever the particular style of the preacher or the age in which he speaks.   He had the passion and the glow of one to whom Christ was the Alpha and the Omega of his faith.

In the end of the day there was no tribute a preacher could covet more than that once paid to Fairbairn when a hearer said, "He himself, rather than what I remember of his speech, was sufficient proof of the existence of the God whose being he was there that night to demonstrate.   That man has seen God face to face."

March 19, 1938

VI

Rev. JOHN McNEILL

YEARS have passed since the death of the Rev. John McNeill.
He had made his name a household word throughout the
English-speaking world, but at the end of all his roaming his body
was brought to rest at last in the little churchyard at Inverkip, not
far from the station where he began life as a railway porter.

The fame of some preachers is evanescent, but that of John
McNeill still stands secure. People come from all parts to see
his grave with its modest, simple stone, and from my correspondence I have reason to know how largely the man and his personality
continue to dominate the minds of many. It is in response to
repeated requests that I am giving some impressions and incidents
which have come to light since my biography of him was published
in 1933. That volume seemed, like the man himself, to have
gone all over the English-speaking world (he had preached almost
everywhere), and its appearance brought letters from readers in
many countries, many of them containing further reminiscences
of John McNeill. What an impression he made by his personality
and preaching, and how lasting has been the memory of some of
his sayings!

John McNeill never tried to hide his humble origin and up-
bringing; he was proud of the fact. One day, after he had risen to
fame, a man was introduced to him. He grasped the man's hand
warmly and exclaimed: "I ken ye fine. I've often taken your
ticket at the station."

"I remember," says a minister, "asking Hugh Black some thirty
years ago, 'Who do you look upon as the greatest living preacher?'
He replied immediately, 'John McNeill.' And at that time
Parker and Whyte and Alexander McLaren were all alive."

There has reached me the following, but of the identity of the
writer I am not certain. He says, "When I was at Blackburn, in
Lancashire, I heard John McNeill when he came to conduct a fortnight's mission there. I heard three or four of his most famous
sermons on that occasion, including 'David in the Dumps,' and
the one about the cleansing of Naaman the Syrian in the Jordan,
from which river he came out no better but a good deal wetter!

"These two addresses were of an almost rollicking kind, but full of good sense, deep sympathy, and strong appeal. I never heard any man who could *appeal* as he could.

"At one of these Blackburn addresses I sat on the platform very near him. I remember how at the beginning of his sermon that night he took his handkerchief out of his pocket—the handkerchief was as needful an accessory to McNeill as a napkin to a waiter. The handkerchief was a fresh one, folded up neatly into a square; as he shook it out he glanced down and saw a large hole in the middle of it. A broad grin at once came over his face, and, poking his finger through the hole, he said with a chuckle, half to himself: 'I'll hae to tell my mither aboot this when I get hame!' And a row of old Lancashire women in the front seat just rocked with merriment."

On one occasion John McNeill convulsed the General Assembly in course of a speech descriptive of his travels and experiences in different parts of the world. The climax came when he told of an incident in a campaign he conducted in Aberdeen.

"Some of the people who were anxious and troubled remained in the church after the service ended. One man who kept his seat in the gallery looked the picture of worry. McNeill told how he went up, sat down in the pew beside him, and asked, 'Can I help you, brother?' The man hesitated for a long time, but ultimately out came the problem which so oppressed him: 'Can ye tell me foo (why) God made the Deevil?' "

In another General Assembly speech he told a story which was greatly enjoyed. "I heard," he said, "of a young minister, maybe a hundred miles from here, and it was his ordination soiree, and he had surrounded himself with seven spirits like himself, young fellows who all told the tale of what a fine fellow this was, and what a student this was, and what a genius this was, and what a good thing it was for the church to have him. And at last the poor fellow believed it himself, and he got up and said that of course he would not be long with them—he was very glad they had called him, and it was a beginning, and it would be a stepping-stone to something better—and so on. And an old elder—one of the dry, wersh, terrible sort—going home said: 'Ay, we'll get that one to bury.'"

From Rev. William Ross, of Edinburgh, there is the following: "The greatest sermon I ever listened to in my life was preached by John McNeill. It was during his Leith campaign, for which I acted as convener and secretary. I was with him at tea in the manse

JAMES CHALMERS

J. G. PATON

Professor
JAMES STALKER

Dr.
ROBERT LAWS

Photo:
LAFAYETTE, Ltd., Glasgow

of Rev. Peter Wilson, and I said, 'You have, I know, a sermon on the rich young ruler. It would be a particular pleasure to hear it.' We sat on till meeting-time at eight o'clock. McNeill did not retire, and we went to the church in a cab.

"He had five minutes of preliminaries: three verses of a hymn and a short prayer. The story of the rich young ruler was read as only John McNeill could read it, and the sermon began.

"It lasted an hour and 40 minutes—it looked more like twenty-five minutes. For sheer naked power I have heard nothing to approach it. John McNeill himself was deeply moved, and apologised, or rather asked to be excused, for carrying his heart on his sleeve for one night for Christ's sake.

"People that I knew to be thoroughly cold and careless wept about me as if their hearts would break. From beginning to end there was no witticism, nothing that could even induce a smile."

The next reminiscence is of a different type. This correspondent says: "I had a party of my office-bearers and their wives in the manse. I was a bachelor then, and my housekeeper had to borrow some cups. I begged the lady, Mrs. Brown, to send plain dishes, but she sent a set of 12 lovely precious cups 250 years old, worth a great deal. During the evening I heard a crash. It was one of the cups—fortunately only one.

"Next evening I was at John McNeill's meeting, so was my housekeeper, unknown to me. His subject that night was 'The Axe that Swam.' In course of his sermon he said, 'It's a queer thing, but true, that it's aye the borrowed thing that get's broken. That cup you borrowed from Mrs. Brown the ither nicht, it was that cup that got broken.'

"Afterwards my housekeeper came to me with tears in her eyes, 'Oh, sir,' she said, 'why did you tell Mr. McNeill about the cup?' I could hardly get her to believe that neither I nor any one else had told him. It was an arrow shot at random, but it certainly found the joint in the armour that night. Mr. McNeill was greatly amused when I did tell him."

It was said by Dr. James Black that he "once heard Principal James Denney, who on occasion could be a precise and caustic critic, remarking at his own table that John McNeill, in dealing with a Bible situation, had a sense of poetry and drama which he himself envied."

To John McNeill's remarkable preaching power, Dr. George Jackson, one of the most experienced and discerning of critics, pays this tribute: "I shall never forget a Sunday afternoon service

which he conducted in Alexander Whyte's church in Edinburgh.
It is more than forty years ago now, but I can still feel the thrill of
that afternoon hour—the Scripture Lesson, the story of the woman
of Samaria, read with a quiet dramatic power that made you feel
as if you were there with Jesus and the woman by the well-side:
the prayer so simple and direct, a strong and gentle man's talk with
God; and then the sermon.

"It was based on the chapter which he had read, and afterwards
it went literally round the world.   As I heard it that afternoon, it
was as unreportable as its power was unmistakable.   The preacher
did not mince his words; at one point towards the close, I remember, he doubled his great fist and told his hearers that they knew he
had hit some of them between the eyes; yet, though he may have
made uneasy consciences squirm, there was nothing coarse or
vulgar in the sermon, nothing that the most fastidious could resent.
Rarely in all my life have I listened to preaching that seemed so
truly the real thing as that afternoon in St. George's."

Great preacher as he was, John McNeill's fame might not still
be so bright if he had not added to his preaching power personal
qualities of no ordinary kind.   He was so genial, so full of wit and
humour, so simple in his tastes and habits, so unassuming and
sympathetic that the more he was known the more he was loved.
The same could not be said of all public men.   Never was he seen
to greater advantage than behind the scenes in his private and
family life.   He used to say that he "would rather see his children's
faces than all the picture galleries of Europe."

A great Evangelical, he was also a great human.   What was said
recently of Rendel Harris could be said with equal truth of John
McNeill, that "he got a 'kick' out of his religion."

July 26, 1941

VII

J. G. PATON and JAMES CHALMERS

OF two missionaries whose names have become household words I have early memories. One was John G. Paton of the New Hebrides, and the other James Chalmers of New Guinea. They were as unlike in many respects as any two men could possibly be, but they were alike in their record of amazing work and in the fascination of their personality.

Both of them had connections with Glasgow, for they began their work as agents of the Glasgow City Mission, as Robert Laws and many others did later on to augment their slender means when preparing for the foreign field. John G. Paton's first appointment was as the teacher in charge of Maryhill Free Church School, where it fell to him to quell the rowdyism which had made it impossible for his three immediate predecessors to carry on their work. Then as an agent of the Glasgow City Mission he was allocated a district in the Calton where he had to break new ground. Soon his influence was felt in many ways, the opposition it aroused being a tribute to its effect. At a very early age he was elected an elder in Dr. Symington's church, and he accepted office when urged to do so by his father and many of his best friends. All this time, to use his own words, he was painfully carrying on his studies, first at Glasgow University, and thereafter at the Reformed Presbyterian Divinity Hall, while also attending medical classes at the Anderson College of Medicine. When he returned from abroad many years later there was scarcely a church in any part of Glasgow where some former member of his Bible Class or old mission worker did not claim his acquaintance.

But he had another and very intimate link with Glasgow through his like-minded brother, Dr. James Paton, of St. Paul's Parish, whose editing of the missionary's autobiography made the world his debtor. James Paton was ahead of his time in the Church of Scotland in temperance and social work, and his interest in the New Hebrides mission was not inferior to that of his famous brother.

When I heard John G. Paton, the snows of many winters were upon him. With his long, flowing beard, his lofty mien and his venerable appearance, he seemed like some patriarch or prophet of old. His name was one to conjure with. Like other youths of the period, I had heard the story of his labours in the New Hebrides until he had become a great heroic figure, and to see him in the flesh and hear the living tones of his voice was an opportunity to be eagerly seized.

As my thoughts go back across the years my main impression of John G. Paton is that of a gracious, benign personality with a quiet, persuasive, compelling influence. He had faced and overcome almost unspeakable obstacles in his work among the heathen, but he conveyed a sense of calm composure rather than of anything dramatic. The story he had to tell, and which he told so simply, would have riveted any audience. But it was the man himself more than anything he said that impressed me. He appeared to have come out of some inner sanctuary, with an aroma about him of things that are sacred and beautiful and uplifting. It was said of John G. Paton when he died that "earth had lost and heaven gained a soul whose life had been an inspiration, and whose memory will be honoured while honour remains among men."

James Chalmers was of quite a different type. He was a full-blooded man of magnificent physique, all aglow with strength and energy. There never was a more perfect embodiment of the muscular Christian.

From Ardrishaig, where he was born, he came to Glasgow, and his district in connection with the Glasgow City Mission was in the High Street. He was a member of Greyfriars' Church under the ministry of Dr. (afterwards Professor) Henry Calderwood, and he worked in some of the agencies of that congregation.

Before he left home he had been a participant in every boyish prank and the leader in many a daring escapade. When he went to Cheshunt College, Cambridge, he remained true to his early reputation—always fond of fun and frolic. His course of study was brief and his training of the slenderest, but any lack in that respect was more than made up for by his great natural gifts. He was a born pioneer missionary, fearless, intrepid, resourceful, and untiring, and in his work among the cannibals of New Guinea he realized the earliest dream of his life.

All the world knows what he was able to accomplish in New Guinea, and he had no more fervent admirer than Robert Louis Stevenson, whom he met in far-off Samoa. The friendship formed between them was strengthened by frequent correspondence, and many of the letters have been published. It is a proof of the opinion

R. L. S. had of Chalmers that he wrote "Your photograph is on my chimney-shelf as large as life."

There was something impressive and compelling in the personality and appearance of James Chalmers. Robert Louis Stevenson spoke of him as a "big, stout, wildish-looking man." He was broad-shouldered and deep-chested, and his face had widened beyond the dimensions of that of Charles Dickens, to whom he had a certain resemblance. I remember in particular his flashing eyes and his magnificent voice.

He had an extraordinary gift of graphic description, scenes and incidents were made to live before the eyes of his hearers. He made you see his struggle with a savage; you held your breath as you seemed to walk with him across the beach to interview a cannibal chief; you saw the wild fierce faces of the natives soften at the story of the Cross, until these men came to sit with him around the Lord's Table.

When I heard Chalmers he was already famous, and although he was no longer young he was full of strength and vigour. There was a great crowded church and an audience which was held spellbound by the personality of the man in the pulpit. Chalmers had only to rise and face a crowd of people and from that moment they were at his feet. There was something about him that was dominating and commanding. His powerful figure, his bushy white mane, his sparkling hazel eyes, his unmistakable air of authority made an immediate and inevitable impression.

But he had also great gifts as a speaker in his own dramatic, vivid way. It has been said of him that he was as restless as a volcano and as subject to eruptions. This was as true of his speaking. To witness the volcanic eruptions of his oratory as he addressed a great gathering was an experience for any listener.

And then he had a marvellous voice. It ranged from exquisite tenderness to imperial command. For the sick, for the old, for anyone who sought his advice in trouble his tones were deep and sympathetic, but his voice could also boom forth with an authority which his colleagues said could restore order in a panic at sea and compel fighting natives to lay down their arms.

I remember how his voice ranged over many notes as he spoke of his work among the heathen, and particularly do I recall the note of victory in it as he spoke of the triumphs of the Cross among the most degraded tribes. He was no faint heart, and although he afterwards perished at the hands of the cannibals he was seeking to save, he had a profound belief that the Christian faith would yet conquer the world. His address—burning, passionate, over-whelming in its power—came to a magnificent and memorable close with the verse, uttered in ringing tones and with an intensity of conviction that stirred the audience as I have seldom seen an audience stirred:

> The beam that shines from Sion hill
> Shall lighten every land ;
> The King who reigns in Salem's tow'rs
> Shall all the world command.

The word "shall" came with a thundering crash which almost brought us from our seats. Never in all my experience have I heard a peroration so thrilling and overwhelming in its effect. Those who were present that night will remember the experience as long as they remember anything.

But it was more than a great oratorical climax. It was a shout of triumph, a passionate and triumphant declaration of faith in the ultimate victory of the Gospel by a man who lived and died in carrying it to the heathen.

January 14, 1938

VIII

Dr. JOSEPH PARKER

THE celebration of the tercentenary of the London City Temple has recalled attention to the great preacher who made it famous—Dr. Joseph Parker.

For 35 years Parker reigned in the City Temple like a king on his throne. At both services on Sunday, and also at his famous Thursday mid-day services, he attracted vast congregations drawn from all classes and from all parts of the world. The back gallery of the City Temple was said to stretch to the Rocky Mountains.

Parker had his peculiarities. Never was there a more shining example of the supreme egoist. Even in his control of the City Temple, he was a law unto himself. He was not only minister of the church, but also its treasurer, and its deacons. The stewards handed him the collection each Sunday, and he paid the expenses and disbursed the money without publishing any accounts. He was the autocrat personified—no one questioned his rule or dared to challenge his decisions.

Around the sayings and doings of this remarkable man there gathered a crop of anecdotes, many of them doubtless apocryphal, some with a grain of truth, and others undeniably true. Mr. Arthur Porritt has told of hearing Dr. Parker say that he hated to speak of money from the pulpit, and he did not believe that habitues of the City Temple meant to evade their duty. "It is all the fault of the fog," he said in his most insinuating tones. "It gets into the church and blurs your eyes, so that when the deacon comes with the collection-box you mistake it for a hymn book, and say, 'No, thank you. I have got one already'."

But the most characteristic thing Mr. Porritt ever heard him say was in a prefatory note to one of his Thursday sermons. He said he approached the duty of preaching that morning with trepidation, because he had had a letter from a gentleman saying that he was coming to the City Temple that day to make a philosophical analysis of the sermon. After a long pause Dr. Parker said, "I may add that my trepidation is somewhat mitigated by the fact that the gentleman spells philosophical with an 'f'."

Daring to a degree at times, Dr. Parker is remembered by some

as the preacher who damned the Sultan.   That dramatic outburst
came after a terrific passage which concluded: "He may have been
the Kaiser's friend, but in the name of God, in the name of the
Father and the Son and the Holy Ghost—speaking of the Sultan
not merely as a man, but speaking of him as the Great Assassin—
I say, 'God damn the Sultan!' "

Less familiar is the incident told by Dr. J. D. Jones.   "Parker,"
he said, "in a tremendous passage, described the Sultan's Armenian
atrocities and the seeming inability of any power to restrain him.
'But,' he declared, 'I believe in another King, our Jesus, whom
Paul affirmed to be alive.'   He shot out that word 'alive' like a
thunderbolt.   It left the audience literally stunned and breathless.
There was a perceptible pause till the people recovered breath.
Then there broke out such a tumult of applause as even the City
Temple had rarely heard."

Above all, Parker was a great preacher.   Neither his personal
idiosyncrasies nor his extraordinary histrionic powers accounted
for the sway he exercised for so many years.   He had, of course,
unusual natural endowments.   His massive figure, and his leonine
head, with its shaggy locks, would have attracted attention anywhere.   The gleaming eyes, the sweeping gestures, the constantly
changing inflexion of his wonderful voice, at one moment like a
roar of thunder and the next soft as a whisper, held any audience
spellbound.   And there was always the element of the unexpected
in what he said and how he said it.   Yet there was something more,
very much more, than all that.   He was a supreme interpreter of
the Scriptures.   His "People's Bible" is a mine for preachers,
because of its freshness and originality and insight.   Often by a
flash of intuition, inspiration, or genius—call it what you will—he
made texts sparkle with a new meaning.

It has been said that he had not the massive intellectual strength
of Dale; he had not the exegetical clearness of Alexander MacLaren;
he had not the perfect artistry of Jowett—he was rough-hewn like
the Northumbria from which he hailed.   He was boisterous, sometimes perhaps bombastic, but he had drama, he had passion, he had
genius, he had great flashes of inspiration which made other
preachers seem dull in comparison.

Dr. Parker made no secret of where he stood as a preacher.
He once published what he called his creed, and among other
statements it contained the following: "I believe there is nothing
worth preaching but the Evangelical faith, though the way of
preaching it is endlessly varied.   I judge no man.   To God every

DR. JOSEPH PARKER

Photo: ERNEST H. MILLS, London

To face page 40

man must make his last appeal.   I preach the love of Christ, the
power of the Cross, the One Priesthood of the One Priest."

His preaching in the pulpit, it has been well said, was "a
spiritual wonder.   There was about it the touch of miracle.
Apparently free from rule, it was unconsciously obedient to the
great principles of art.   As you listened you saw deeper meanings.
The horizon lifted, widened, broadened—the preacher had thrust
his hand among your heartstrings.   You heard the cry of life, and
the Christ preached as answer to that cry.   The preacher had
every gift.   He was mystical, poetical, ironical, rebuking, by
turns.   Sometimes

As from an infinitely distant land,
Come airs and floating echoes that convey
A melancholy into all our day.

The next moment you could not help smiling at some keen witticism.   Then he was ironical, and you remembered Heine, and
saw that he knew how much irony is mingled by God in the order
of his creation.   Then tears sprang to your eyes as he pictured the
failure of success, and told of the long triumphant struggle and the
victory turned into mourning by the death of the only child.   But
what description can render, or what analysis explain, the visible
inspiration, the touch of fire from heaven?"

I am glad and thankful to have heard Joseph Parker.   No name
is more secure than his among British preachers on the roll of fame.

April 26, 1940

IX

Professor JAMES STALKER

IT has always seemed a pity that we have had no biography of Professor Stalker, who was so much of a personality and whose gifts were so distinctive. He filled a large place in the religious life of this country and he was more widely known in America than any other Scottish preacher of his day.

Although he spent twenty of the later years of his life as a professor, it is as a preacher we still think of him. And it was by his two remarkable handbooks (still unsurpassed in their own way) on the "Life of Christ" and the "Life of St. Paul," and by his preaching, that he made his name famous.

Of his ministries in St. Brycedale, Kirkcaldy, and St. Matthew's, Glasgow, there are many memories and traditions. Some can still recall how he made St. Matthew's resound with preaching which, in its boldness in regard to social and other questions, caused some douce hearers to become uneasy. In the pulpit in those days he was in the fulness of his strength and glorying in his work.

Of Stalker in St. Matthew's it has been written: "A smallish figure, with a squareness of shoulder underneath the draping gown, comes from a side door, and immediately, above red pulpit cushions, appears a face that carries out the suggestion already given. Man and manner, there is a sturdiness and seriousness, painstaking, absorbed, with some *brusquerie,* and again some nervousness. The face strikes you. It is an oblong, divided by two dark lines—the straight and marked eyebrows, the moustache turning iron-grey. The dark hair, also greying, lies flat upon and away from the head. Ill-hung, but vigorous, are the mouth and jaw, and the voice corresponds. It is weighty, but not sweet; nothing lingers in the ear, captivating you in spite of yourself. This man takes you as a man, more than an artist, although he is not without touches of the latter."

That voice of his had something of a bark in it; it was as brusque as his manner often was. The sort of shout with which he would begin a service was somewhat disconcerting to those hearing him for the first time.

A story is often told of his St. Matthew's days. It had been almost his invariable custom to begin the service with a prayer of thanksgiving. There came a wet, foggy day when Glasgow was at its worst, and he had been wending his way to church under the dreariest conditions. Everyone was feeling miserable and wondering what he would do that morning. Up the pulpit stairs he went, and, as the people waited anxiously, he began in his quick, abrupt way: "We thank Thee, O Lord, that every day is not like this."

Stalker, like Henry Drummond, was one of those who shared in the revival movement which followed the Moody and Sankey mission of 1873, and he was, after Drummond, perhaps the most active of the youthful enthusiasts of the time. The experience left a lasting effect upon him. "At that time," he said, "we had many experiences which have ever since made Christ intelligible; and the Book of the Acts of the Apostles especially has a meaning to those who have passed through such a movement which it could scarcely, I should think, have for anyone else."

The Evangelical glow of those early days remained with Stalker ever after. It was felt in all his preaching; it gave him an interest in every movement, however humble, to carry the Gospel to the people. Even in old age he maintained a keen interest in aggressive work of all kinds—religious and social.

In the pulpit he never had his full manuscript; he contented himself with half a sheet of notepaper which he lifted up to consult openly at the beginning of each of his "heads." To all intents he was an extempore preacher, facing his hearers and enjoying perfect freedom in manner and delivery. As a preacher he was once compared to a blacksmith. "The dark, strong energy of the moderate figure," said Deas Cromarty, "was like that of a man at the anvil, using force but measuring it, driving at a point but guarding the blow."

I never heard Stalker preach without being impressed by his lucidity. He was, indeed, so lucid that he did not always get credit for the ability that was behind it all. There was "body" in his preaching; his diction could often be vivid and picturesque; but, above all, there was that steady sequence of thought, that orderly march of argument, to what seemed the inevitable conclusion. He was a great believer in the practice of "heads" or divisions—a practice which many of us regret is not so common to-day as it once was.

Perhaps one of the best examples of Stalker's style of preaching was found in his sermon on Christ as "The Advocate," which was afterwards published. It was founded on the incident when Mary, the friend of Christ, "had performed one of those actions which, scattered at rare intervals along the tracts of time, indicate the emergence of new powers in human nature; but so much was it misunderstood and misjudged that, had not Jesus intervened, it would either have been consigned to oblivion or remembered as a scandal. The Advocate, however, was on the spot. It was a woman that had been attacked; and all the chivalry of His nature rose up to protect her. There is unmistakable heat in His first words, 'Let her alone; why trouble ye her?' And then His strokes fall, blow after blow of argument and rebuke, on the heads of her opponents, till she is not only vindicated, but raised on a pedestal for the admiration and imitation of all generations."

Then there came his characteristically striking divisions.

(1) In thus vindicating His friend, Jesus was vindicating the Beautiful against the Useful. "She hath wrought a good work on me," for the word translated "good" is literally "beautiful."

(2) In defending His friend, Jesus was vindicating the Original against the Conventional. "The poor ye have always with you, but me ye have not always."

(3) In defending His friend, Jesus was vindicating the Particular against the General. "She hath done what she could."

(4) In defending His friend, Jesus was vindicating the Conscious against the Unconscious. "She is come aforehand to anoint my body to the burying."

The sermon closed with these sentences: "Thorny was the bed on which Jesus lay down, yet it was smoothed to roses by love. Thus did the fragrance of Mary's ointment float round the cross, and that was fulfilled which had been written of old, 'He shall see of the travail of his soul and shall be satisfied'."

Stalker was never afraid to speak his mind fearlessly and frankly. At the settlement of a friend to the pastorate of a wealthy West-End congregation in Glasgow he said: "If you make my friend a typical West-End minister, great at dinner-parties and in smoking rooms, and a preacher of smooth things to them that are in ease in Zion, this will be the saddest day of his life."

He had a high conception of the ministry. In an induction charge he once said: "I like to think of the minister as only one of the congregation set apart by the rest for a particular purpose. They say to him: Look, brother, we are busy with our daily toils, and confused with cares, but we eagerly long for peace and light to illuminate our life, and we have heard there is a land where these are to be found, a land of repose and joy, full of thoughts that breathe and words that burn, but we cannot go thither ourselves. We are too embroiled in daily cares. Come, we will elect you, and set you free from toil, and you shall go thither for us, and week by week trade with that land and bring us its treasures and its spoils."

Powerful in the pulpit, he could at times be thrilling on the platform, as Glasgow had reason to know on many a memorable occasion. Once he even surpassed Lord Rosebery. It was at a great gathering held in Glasgow in connection with social work. "The speakers on that occasion," it was said, "were carefully chosen, but the two speeches of the evening were those of Lord Rosebery and Dr. Stalker. There were deep notes of passion and of pathos in the address of the statesman which were absent from that of the minister, but there was no speech that reached the great audience and roused it as Stalker's did."

Personal ambition did not seem to trouble him. He declined a Principalship on the ground of age, and gladly worked under a younger man; and he refused nomination to the Moderatorship. Tales are told of his brusque manner, but beneath the seemingly gruff exterior there was a warm heart. Speaking for myself, I always found him the soul of courtesy, and I have grateful memories of his kindness. He often went out of his way to do a brotherly deed.

I conclude with what Dr. George Jackson said of Stalker's "Life of Christ"—words as true as when they were written many years ago: "The ease, the lucidity, the crystalline clearness with which the familiar story is retold are the last result of years of patient study and deep meditation. Dr. Stalker writes clearly because he sees clearly. The dead past has lived again before him; and it lives still for us in these graphic, vivid pages. Yet, throughout, the imagination works under wise restraints. The small canvas is never overcrowded. The leading facts of the history are seized and fixed with a master hand; the rest is forgotten. In nothing is the touch of the true literary artist more clearly seen than in the skill with which the writer has first selected and then grasped his materials. His book is a miracle of condensation, a miniature masterpiece."

April 23, 1938

X

LAWS OF LIVINGSTONIA

"THERE is a prince and a great man fallen this day in Israel." That was the universal feeling when the news became known of the death of Dr. Robert Laws. He was frequently referred to as the greatest living missionary, and now that he is dead his name is assured of an enduring place on the roll of fame. He will rank with those great Scots missionary pioneers, John G. Paton of the New Hebrides, and the martyred James Chalmers of New Guinea, and even with David Livingstone, whose mantle fell upon his shoulders. And it is not as a missionary only that he will be remembered. He was of the race of Empire builders whose services were recognised by the King, acknowledged by the Government, and applauded by the nation.

It is, said one who knew him well, the bare truth that he was unique amongst missionary pioneers, administrators, and statesmen. In variety of attainments, in capacity for all forms of work, in indomitable faith and patience, and in magnificent practical achievement no one has surpassed him. He was a super-missionary. He possessed as much courage as David Livingstone, and certainly as much faith and endurance. There was no more touching sight in Africa, the writer continued, than the old white-headed Doctor, after a lifetime of adventure and achievement, issuing from the manse before six o'clock in the morning and disappearing into the mist which still shrouded the mountain; toiling at all sorts of professional and manual work throughout the day, and coming back tired in the twilight—and so unconscious of the heroism of it.

It is not my intention to traverse the facts, so full of thrilling romance, in the career of Dr. Laws. Mr. W. P. Livingstone's classic biography and his more recent volume for boys, "The Hero of the Lake," have made everyone so familiar with the story that it is unnecessary to recapitulate the details. I am rather to give some personal recollections and impressions of Dr. Laws as he was known to me over a long period of years.

Of his father I have an early boyhood memory. He was spared to a green old age and had the joy of seeing his only son honoured in the Church and famous throughout the world. "Old Robert Laws," as everyone affectionately and reverently called him, was as saintly a man as ever walked the earth. As his son said of him, he was "an Israelite indeed, in whom is no guile." Venerable in appearance, gracious in manner, he went about doing good in his own quiet way. Few men had such a remarkable gift in prayer. His voice became subdued and yet vibrant with emotion as he bowed in adoring worship and poured forth quietly and with simple confidence and prevailing faith his earnest intercessions.

The influence of such a father meant more than could ever be reckoned. "Old Robert Laws" lived again in his son, and the Church and the world are debtors to that unknown saint.

No one could ever claim for Dr. Laws that he had any special gifts as a speaker. His personality certainly never failed to impress an audience, for everyone could sense that a great man and a master worker was speaking. But his addresses in themselves had neither frills nor thrills. He seemed as indifferent to rhetoric as he was incapable of it, and he told his tale in a bare, unadorned way, leaving the facts to speak for themselves. Yet I can recall one occasion when he was unconsciously dramatic.

It was in the church of his boyhood, and he was urging his youthful hearers to value their privileges and not to neglect their church attendance. Then, pausing and pointing with uplifted hand, he continued: "In my first years in Central Africa, when there was no church bell to remind me it was Sunday morning, and the only sounds were the shrieks of the natives and the howl of the wild beasts, I would see in my thoughts the back of this pulpit as I had so often seen it as a boy, and I would be strengthened and comforted in my loneliness among the heathen." It was a simple statement, uttered in broken and faltering accents, but its unstudied effect was thrilling to a degree.

Nothing impressed me more about Dr. Laws than his humility. He was a great man who was unconscious of his greatness. It is true that he could never have accomplished the work he did unless he had been possessed of a dominating personality. He was masterful in his way, with a certain dour, dogged Scots persistence. Perhaps he could even be autocratic in his methods. But there was never a more humble-minded man nor one who had less thought of his own glory. "No, no, no!" he exclaimed when reference was made to the transformation he had effected in Central Africa. "You must not put me in the foreground. God has used me for His purpose, and I am grateful, but I want no credit." And that was not the protest of a mock humility which can be so easily seen through. It had the true ring of an honest and humble soul.

High and low in the social scale were all alike to Dr. Laws. He would neither fawn on the one nor forget the other. When he was Moderator of the General Assembly—an honour he was prevailed on to accept only because it would help the mission cause—his Moderatorial reception was attended by Mr. Lloyd George, then Chancellor of the Exchequer. But there was another guest specially invited by the Moderator, his old landlady in Edinburgh, who had been so careful in the management of his meagre resources when he was a Divinity student that he declared she was a more remarkable and certainly a more economical chancellor of the exchequer than the other.

Since he retired, none too willingly, from the mission field, and settled in Edinburgh, Dr. Laws had been constant in his attendance at the meetings of the General Assembly, where he was always one of the figures of the greatest interest. "Laws of Livingstonia," members would whisper to one another, as his venerable form was seen in the Hall, and in the public galleries people would stand up to see one who was by common consent the "Grand Old Man" of the Church. Of all the interest he aroused he was sublimely ignorant, and he moved about the corridors as unobtrusively as the most inconspicuous minister or elder from the country.

One incident at this year's Assembly will be a happy memory to all who witnessed it. It was the opening day, and a crowded House awaited the appearance of the Lord High Commissioner in the Throne Gallery. Almost at the last moment, Dr. Laws appeared and, when he was looking for a place on the crowded rostrum, Dr. White, the Leader of the House, with a fine instinct, went and took the veteran's arm and placed him in the seat of honour at the right hand of the Moderator. It was an act and a recognition which caused a murmur of approval throughout the Assembly. The right man, it was felt, was in the right place. Honour had been paid where honour was due. If it had been known it was to be his last Assembly, nothing could have been finer or more fitting.

Dr. Laws had left Edinburgh recently for London to be with his daughter and only child, now herself a graduate in medicine, Dr. Amelia Nyasa Laws, and he had been enjoying the garden of the house she had taken at Ealing. On Wednesday of last week when at the British Museum, still eager in his quest, he became

Principal
JOHN CAIRNS

Photo:
T. & R. ANNAN, Glasgow

Dr.
JOHN HUNTER

Photo:
T. & R. ANNAN, Glasgow

To face page 48

Rev. C.
SILVESTER HORNE

Photo:
REGINALD HAINES, London

Principal
JAMES MORISON

Photo:
JOHN FERGUS, Largs

suddenly ill, but was able to reach his daughter's rooms. He was kept under careful medical observation for two days, and on Friday an eminent consulting surgeon was called in. The surgeon considered it unwise to operate because of Dr. Laws' advanced age, but on Saturday the trouble became more localised, and he suggested that the patient be given the option of an operation. With the calm courage with which he had faced many a crisis in his life Dr. Laws faced this last crisis of all. Calmly and characteristically he replied, "The surgeon knows best. Let it be done."

But recovery was not to be. He had lived quietly all his life and now as quietly he passed away. Yet for him all the trumpets must have sounded on the other side.

Unostentatious in life, it cannot be said that his death was other than what he himself might have wished. He had often slipped away from a crowded meeting to escape recognition and applause. So he slipped away at last before the public even knew of his illness. It was only next day that the world awoke to the fact that it had lost one of the great figures of this generation.

His work was done; he had fought a good fight; he had kept the faith; and he could say with Simeon of old, "Lord, now lettest thou thy servant depart in peace . . . for mine eyes have seen Thy salvation." To him it had been granted to witness the coming of his Lord in the Africa he loved.

> *Now the labourer's task is o'er,*
> *Now the battle-day is past;*
> *Now upon the further shore*
> *Lands the voyager at last.*

August 11, 1934

4

XI

Dr. JOHN HUNTER

THERE was a time when the name of John Hunter may have been said to be a household word in Glasgow. It stood for something more than that of a local Congregational minister; it stood, indeed, for one of the leading pulpit personalities of his time whose influence, both in the city and far beyond its bounds, reached out beyond all denominational limitations.

John Hunter had other ministries in York and in Hull, and, later on, for a time in King's Weigh House Church, London—but it was in Trinity Church, Glasgow, that he rose to the full height of his power. He was minister there from 1887 till 1901, and again from 1904 till 1913. There were other preachers of note in the city during those years—men whose names are still remembered—but Hunter filled a place peculiarly his own.

I have many memories of him, particularly as he was in the days of his prime. He made a striking and distinctive figure in the pulpit. The clean-shaven face, with its austere aspect, might have been that of some divine whose portrait had been handed down from a former generation. In his youth as a preacher he had disdained the use of pulpit gowns, but he changed his opinion on that matter, a change which some regarded as typical of his altered attitude on other and more important matters. Certainly he developed, with the passing years, a liking for something more studied and orderly, and perhaps more ornate, in the form of service, just as there became apparent a gradual leaning towards what was popularly known as a broader theology. Of the former there was proof in his special arrangement for the order of service in his own church, while his change in the latter aspect was revealed in his occasional outbursts against a form of Evangelicalism which in his younger days he was understood to accept.

His pulpit style was not modelled on that of anyone else; it was in every sense his own. His voice had very small compass, and such as it was, he did not use it to the best effect. The opening hymn was announced abruptly and almost inaudibly. The prayer would open in the same tone, and strangers hearing him for the first time would begin to wonder wherein his power lay. By and by, however, some impressive petition would fall on the ear; the congregation would be gradually hushed until every devout worshipper felt the encircling of a spiritual atmosphere; and even the careless could remain no longer untouched. His prayers were not the mere repetition of well-worn petitions. They abounded in arresting and memorable phrases, and while at times they may have partaken of religious musing, at others they were very definite in supplication and intercession.

Here it may be remarked that his volume of "Devotional Services for Public Worship" ran through edition after edition, and ministers of all denominations have found suggestion and inspiration in its pages. There are those who hold that it is by this book of prayers that Hunter's fame will be most lasting.

The power of the man in the pulpit was revealed most of all in the sermon. I can still see him as he steadily and surely established his mastery over his hearers. He began quietly. The voice was pitched in the same key throughout, but in the gathering stillness, amid the tense attention of the congregation, it began to ring out sharp and clear, especially when he reached a climax in his argument. The gestures were few—perhaps only once or twice was an arm raised—but then it was at the right moment and it was not only effective but dramatic.

Who that ever witnessed it can forget one of John Hunter's passionate outbursts. He may have stood reading page after page from his manuscript almost as motionless as a statue and with scarcely an inflexion in his tones. Then, at a certain passage, his figure would suddenly become transformed, with the eyes flashing, the lips quivering, the voice piercing in its intensity, the whole man vibrating with passion. It was at moments like these that he gave his hearers such a thrill that they declared they felt pins and needles in the spine. It is no wonder that he was described by one of his contemporaries as "the greatest master of manuscript preaching."

Solidity was one of the outstanding features of Dr. Hunter's sermons. Hard thinking and close reasoning were apparent from first to last. Every word and phrase told as he built up a strong and stately fabric. His language was terse and telling, and he introduced many a gem from classical and current literature which delighted his youthful hearers in particular.

God in His majesty and His mercy; man in his unrest and his yearning for the Divine; the soul in its priceless and imperishable worth; materialism in its degrading and deadening influence; duty in its rigid imperativeness—these were themes on which he delighted to dwell and aspects of truth to which he again and again returned.   It may be that the Atonement of Christ was not so often on his lips as the Fatherhood of God.   But he had such a vivid sense of God himself—it was said to be more real to him than anything else—that he was able to communicate something of it to his hearers.

In the biography by his son (now Bishop of Sheffield) it is well said that "when he let his thought gather round some great affirmation like 'the Eternal God is thy refuge, and underneath are the everlasting arms,' or 'The Living God,' or 'Whom have I in Heaven but Thee, and there is none upon earth that I desire beside Thee,' or 'This is my God and I will praise Him, my Father's God and I will exalt Him,' or the Aaronic Benediction, or 'the first and great Commandment,' or Psalms like the 23rd or the 139th—one felt that he had entered intimately into the experience which lay behind the words of the text.   And the memory of the actual words of his discourse would often be effaced by the sense of God's reality and presence which he had induced."

John Hunter held to his convictions, and proclaimed without fear or favour the truth as he had known and experienced it in his own soul.   Perhaps nothing finer was ever spoken of him than by his friend from early days, Principal P. T. Forsyth, in his funeral tribute, in course of which he said: "He belonged to the great race of prophet and apostle.   He was in some ways a free-lance among men—whose point was always sunk before God—one as apt to pray as powerful to preach, who reached men always because he always touched God.   He waited on God and not on man.   He had great gifts—but from first to last he worked always as if he had none.   He was a furious toiler both before the pulpit and in it. He had the austerity of a rich nature, but there was the austerity which did not commend him to all.   He was impatient, and even intractable, like some of the first figures of faith, in the face of moral stupidity sicklied with religious sentiment and easy egoism.   His prophetic soul rose above crude sentiment, yet he never lost warm feeling for men; and he was rich in spiritual feeling, deep, solemn, and shy."

That was Dr. John Hunter as we knew him.

July 9, 1938

XII

GENERAL BOOTH

TO have heard General William Booth was a great experience.
That the founder of The Salvation Army was a figure who will
live in history, there can be no manner of doubt. Whatever may
be thought of the man or his methods, the fact remains that he will
stand with Wesley and others who initiated movements with a
revolutionary effect on the religious life of their time, and have
left an abiding and worldwide influence.

It was impossible to see or hear the General without being
impressed by the sheer power of his dominating personality.
There was something hypnotic in the spell he cast over his fellow
men whether singly or in crowds. Masterful was the term often
applied to him, and not unjustly. But he was not only masterful in
his methods; he was masterful in his whole appearance and bearing.
As his piercing eyes looked out from above his long patriarchal
white beard, he seemed like the reincarnation of some prophet of
olden time.

In some respects his personality was a complex one. I remember a writer who went to interview him in his office many
years ago saying that he expected to meet a visionary and saint,
and he found the astutest business man in the city. "You feel,"
said this interviewer, "that if the tradesman's son of Nottingham
had applied himself to winning wealth instead of to winning souls,
he would have become the Rockefeller of England. He would
have engineered 'corners' and 'squeezes' without precedent.
He would have made the world of finance tremble at his nod.
When he passes by the Stock Exchange, he must say 'there but
for the grace of God goes William Booth.'"

That he had a certain genius for affairs was seen by the fabric
of his creation—the network of social and regenerative agencies
with which he overspread the world. Those who knew him best
found him very acute and able, a practical and hard-headed man
of affairs. The late Lord Wolseley once described him as the
greatest organiser in the world. Like Wesley he combined the
genius for great conceptions with the genius for practical detail.

Along with this, it was admitted, even by his friends, he

was something of a showman. He made a noise in the world, it has been said, not only because it served a perfectly righteous purpose, but because it was his nature to attract attention and arouse interest. He was hotly indignant when persecutions were cruel and malicious, but for the ordinary attacks and criticisms of the world he was always ready with the defence of good-humoured laughter. "They only help to advertise us," he would say. Any man who wanted to "bang his drum" for him was welcome to do so. The great thing with him in those days was to keep the drum beating, to be for ever in the public eye, to be for ever a vital and striking part of national existence. His wisdom told him that a great spiritual offensive must "never degenerate into the appearance of a truce."

Yet, when all is said about General Booth's keen business instincts, his skill in organisation, and his tendency to "beat the drum," the man behind all that was at heart a flaming evangelist. He began as an evangelist, and through all the developments of his social and humanitarian schemes he never lost his evangelical fire or fervour. And it is of General Booth as a preacher that I have personal recollections.

It has to be remembered that he had no regular course of training. He graduated in the rough-and-tumble oratory of the streets. His knowledge of theology was admittedly very limited. In the quarrels of creeds he was not interested. Literature made no appeal to him. He saw men and women as sinners needing to be saved from a Hell in which he believed to the end of his life. So he concentrated every power of which he was possessed in seeking to snatch them from the jaws of something worse than death. From first to last he was a revivalist. To him there were no realities so demonstrable as the realities of the spiritual world— most of all the reality of Christ's real personal presence and saving power. He found, it has been said, that unquestioning faith in Christ's power worked everywhere and under all conditions.

By the time I heard him, the General was already an old man. His voice had suffered from constant use, particularly in the open air. It was as rasping as a saw; some one described it as "a queer, worn, torn, corncrake voice." But the passion vibrating in every tone made it powerful and impressive.

A description of him at this period may be quoted: "Tall and attenuated, with slightly stooping shoulders, the frail body of the man would have seemed almost feeble but for the vigour and distinction of the strong head. His hair, which was snow-white, grew long, and was brushed carelessly, standing up from the brow and falling backwards to the neck and ears. His face was almost bloodless in its pallor. The rather small eyes, under dark and restless eyebrows, had the brightness of beads. The lower part of his face was covered by a moustache and beard as white as his hair. It seemed as if he were a figure carved out of chalk. In repose, he was like a tired man who observes and reflects between spells of nodding sleep, but in action, with his thin arms raised above his head, his eyes blazing, and his powerful voice hurtling out his thoughts, he was like a prophet."

One could never forget how he strode the platform, imperious and dominating, on fire with a consuming passion. He used to say that he liked his tea as he liked his religion—hot, and it was always a hot religion he preached.

"Look!" he cried in one of his addresses, "Look at that man yonder; look at him going down the river. There he is going down in a boat with Niagara beyond. He has got out into the stream; the rapids have got hold of the boat, and down he goes. He need not pull at the oars; he has nothing to do but to be still; to go on with his sleep; to go on with his novel. He is going— going—going. My God! he is gone over, and he never pulled at an oar. That is the way people are damned; they go on; they are preoccupied; they are taken up; they have no time; they don't think; they neglect salvation, and they are lost."

He could be dramatically sensational in order to startle and even shock people out of their indifference. Some of the things he did can never be forgotten. He would picture Lot going out to warn his sons-in-law on the last night in Sodom, and would turn up his coat-collar, and seize somebody's hat to suggest a man going out on a disagreeable but imperious errand, and the whole audience would be given the feeling of the dark night, the knocking at the door, the coming doom, and then the hollow laughter of the young men.

His son and successor, Bramwell Booth, has said that he had seen thousands of people transfixed as the General spoke of the various classes of sinners suffering their doom in the regions of the lost, and one among them counting, always counting—"One— two—three—four—five—then ten—eleven—twelve—thirteen— until you could have heard the drop of the proverbial pin—as he came to "twenty-eight—twenty-nine—thirty. Why, it is JUDAS!"

His appeal was always to the heart and conscience, and his vocabulary was that of the common people—clear, direct, vigorous, simple. It was a dictum of his: "Use words that Mary Ann will understand, and you will be sure to make yourself clear to her mistress; whereas if you speak only to her mistress, you will very likely miss her, and Mary Ann as well."

He made no attempt to instruct or edify. In his preaching to general audiences all over the world his one and direct message was that of Jesus Christ and His Salvation, and his single aim to bring men and women to decision. He was, it has been said, a messenger to the heart of mankind—a courier taking the most direct route, and making all possible haste.

Never surely was there a greater romance in real life than that of William Booth, who, from being persecuted, sneered at, pilloried in every way, in the early days of his Salvation Army, lived to be received by his Sovereign, to be presented with the freedom of the City of London, and to be one of the heroes of his time and a figure of worldwide fame. But, just as adversity never made him swerve from his high purpose, popularity failed to turn his head.

He had his limitations, his weaknesses, his human frailties. But he was more tender-hearted than his leonine appearance and his autocratic methods would have led one to believe. Nor was he without a saving sense of humour. On his deathbed, when his end was near and he was giving his farewell messages to his son, who was to be his successor as General of the Salvation Army, he said to him almost with a chuckle: "I'm leaving you a bonny handful!"

The photograph is the one which was seized upon by The Salvation Army as the truest likeness of their General. Gentleness and tenderness had by that time given a beauty of its own to the old and rugged face. "In that face," it has been said, "one can see how the spirit was bowed down by the sorrows and sufferings of humanity. There is nothing there of the thundering preacher, or the vigorous 'showman,' or the burning prophet, but only the infinite compassion of an old man for a world which is unhappy, a world for which he had toiled all his days."

June 22, 1940

GENERAL BOOTH

To face page 56

XIII

Principal JOHN CAIRNS

IT still stirs one's heart to think of John Cairns, with his massive personality, his strength and his simplicity, his real greatness, and, not least, his unconquerable modesty. The shepherd's son had made such a place for himself that at the age of forty he had the Principalship of Edinburgh University within his grasp, but immediately declined that influential position on the ground that he had consecrated himself to the service of Christ in the Church. That decision was remarkable in itself, but far more noteworthy and characteristic was the fact that he mentioned the offer to no one, and even his brothers knew nothing of it until they were going through his correspondence after his death. Is there another such instance on record anywhere?

John Cairns was a man of one ministry, his only charge being at Berwick-on-Tweed, where he spent over 30 years. But scarcely a year passed without overtures or calls reaching him from churches elsewhere. Many of these he nipped in the bud and went quietly on his way without making public reference to them. Occasionally, however, in spite of all his efforts, a congregation would proceed with a call and he was faced with the necessity of making a decision in public. This was the case when Greyfriars' Church, Glasgow, sought his services. Glasgow had always been regarded as the headquarters of the United Presbyterian Church, and Greyfriars' was then its leading congregation in the city. It was argued that, in the interests of the denomination at large, it was his duty to accept. This was a crisis in his career. After much searching of heart he decided to remain at Berwick, and when he announced this to his congregation in a crowded church it was said that the old building echoed with a sound in which one "could not discern the shout of joy from the noise of the weeping of the people."

When he did leave Berwick it was not to go to another charge but to give his whole time as a Professor in the United Presbyterian Theological Hall in Edinburgh, of which shortly afterwards he was appointed Principal. Thus he became Principal John Cairns, the name by which he was universally known to the end of the chapter.

My first impression of him as a preacher was when, as a boy, I was taken to hear him on one of the many occasions on which he was conducting some special or anniversary service. I was too young then to form any impression of his sermon, but I can recall the crowded church, the tense expectancy of the congregation, the thrill which seemed to pass over it as the venerable figure entered the pulpit, and its eager, rapt response to his powerful preaching. Later on I had other opportunities of hearing him when I could appreciate something of his wonderful influence.

I can still see him as he appeared in the pulpit. A big man physically, as well as in every other sense, "his back was bent as if waiting for a burden and his neck was swathed into stiffness by the coils of a black silk stock." A shock of white hair crowned his head, and he had the bushy side-whiskers of his time. It was not in any artifice of deportment that he excelled, for there was always something awkward about his movements.

But his arms seemed to give him most trouble. They were long, powerful arms and apparently difficult to dispose of when he was in the pulpit. His mother said, "Oor John wull aye be wampishin' wi' his airms." And this was certainly true. When he warmed to his theme the great arms began to swing round and round with a strength that would have laid a man low. It was all utterly ungainly, and it would have been enough to wreck the pulpit popularity of most men. But in his case it was quite otherwise. Once we were under his preaching spell, the great sweep of arm which punctuated each period seemed to become so natural that we would have missed it if it hadn't been there.

Of his voice one can only say that it was strong and telling rather than melodious or pleasing. It had no studied cadences, indeed it violated nearly every rule of elocution. And yet there was something in it, and the way he used it, that made people declare they would have walked miles just to hear John Cairns say, "Let us pray."

The sermon of his of which I have the most vivid memory was on "the bright and morning star." To this day I never read or hear the verse, "I am the root and the offspring of David and the bright and morning star," but I think of the great sermon I heard on it by John Cairns. He rolled out again and again "the bright and morning star" in reverberating tones which one could never forget. It was a sermon he took around with him for special occasions, for, like more modern preachers, he had his "travellers." Other favourites of his own, as also of his hearers, were on "His enemies

shall be clothed with shame," and "Behold, He is alive for evermore." Most of his sermons followed the old Scottish tradition
—"a lengthy introduction, three or four heads, and a twofold
conclusion addressing Gospel invitations to the unconverted and
Gospel assurances to the converted."

Massive as was the preaching of John Cairns, in keeping with
his extraordinary intellectual power, and perfect as an example of
rugged oratory, it was, after all, his personality that was the chief
secret of his influence. That is why I believe his preaching, while
it might not conform to modern standards, would be as telling
to-day as it was then. If ever the power of personality was felt
in preaching, it was in the case of John Cairns. His transparent
goodness, his simplicity of character, his forgetfulness of self shone
through every utterance. He was a saint who was unconscious of
his saintliness, and thus, by voice and pen, he exercised a greater
influence than he ever knew.

"To sum up," said "W. R. N.," many years ago, "John Cairns
was a living proof and illustration of the words of the Shorter
Catechism which was so dear to him: 'The benefits which in this
life do accompany or flow from justification, adoption, and sancti-
fication are assurance of God's love, peace of conscience, joy in
the Holy Ghost, increase of grace, and perseverance therein to the
end'."

When John Cairns lay on his deathbed, his strong mind wandered—wandered back to public scenes in which he had taken part,
and he was heard to murmur words familiar to those who had gone
with him from ante-rooms to public platforms: "You go first, I
follow." It was perhaps his most characteristic saying, and it is a
story which cannot be too often told. It revealed the humility of
true greatness.

October 2, 1937

XIV

Dr. J. H. JOWETT

"THE greatest preacher in the English-speaking world" was a description not infrequently applied to J. H. Jowett when he was in the fulness of his strength. Both in his own country and in America his pulpit influence was one of the most potent of his time.

Jowett was an Englishman, with many of the characteristics of his native Yorkshire, but he owed something to Scotland. He was a student in Arts at Edinburgh University, which afterwards conferred upon him the honorary degree of D.D. But in Edinburgh he received more than his University education. He came under the spell of Henry Drummond and served as one of the stewards at his students' meetings, while he revelled in the opportunity of hearing some of the notable preachers who were then in Edinburgh pulpits. Dr. George Matheson, the blind poet-preacher of St. Bernard's; Dr. John Pulsford, the mystic, in Albany Street Congregational Chapel; Dr. Landels, in Dublin Street Baptist Church; and, above all, Dr. Alexander Whyte, then at his best, in Free St. George's, drew him as with a magnet. For Dr. Whyte he always had a special reverence.

With the West of Scotland Jowett also had a connection. His favourite holiday resort above all others was the Island of Arran, and he came there year after year. For Corrie he had a particular affection.

The main facts of Jowett's life are well known—his first ministry in Newcastle; his famous ministry at Carr's Lane, Birmingham, where he succeeded Dr. R. W. Dale; his term in Fifth Avenue Church, New York, and his last years in Westminster Chapel, London. He preached his last sermon in December, 1922, and, after a period of failing health, died a year later at the age of 60. It was a tragic loss, and one of the first messages of sympathy received by Mrs. Jowett within an hour or two of the news becoming known was from King George V., who said that "through his personal acquaintance with Dr. Jowett he could well realize how deeply his loss would be mourned by all who experienced the power of his great spiritual influence and guidance."

DR. J. H. JOWETT

To face page 60

The first time I heard Jowett preach was in the Metropolitan Tabernacle, London, the scene of C. H. Spurgeon's great ministry. It was a trying test for any man to stand where Spurgeon stood, and few could have faced the ordeal as Jowett did. His fame had attracted a congregation which filled the huge auditorium. After the area and gallery had been filled, the second gallery was opened and into it also the people continued to pour in a steady stream until it was estimated there was a crowd of about 5000. What a sea of faces confronted the preacher as he looked out from the platform pulpit.

On other occasions, and under more average conditions, I heard Jowett in Scotland. There was always a crowded church, for the people flocked to hear him wherever he went. But it was different from preaching in the Tabernacle, where the shadow of Spurgeon seemed ever to hover over the place. It was easier to study the man and his methods where there was not always that sense of another preacher's presence.

I do not think it could be said there was anything peculiarly fascinating or enthralling about Jowett's appearance in the pulpit. His personality exuded no pensive charm. Instead of being absorbed in dreamy wistfulness he was alert and purposeful in every fibre of his being. It has been said that he would have passed for a prosperous solicitor or a medical specialist in a good Harley Street practice. While entirely discarding clerical attire, he was fastidious about his personal appearance and was as immaculate in his dress as Henry Drummond. His easy competence for the task he had in hand; his control of himself at every moment—these were always apparent.

It was, perhaps, his control of himself in the pulpit which prevented him from exercising over his hearers that overmastering, overwhelming effect of some other preachers. He did not allow himself to be irresistibly carried away, and therefore he did not carry others away as if on a flood against which there could be no resistance. I cannot say that he ever thrilled me to the depths as I have been thrilled in rare moments under some preaching. But for sheer mastery of pulpit technique I never listened to anyone who could surpass or even equal Jowett. In craftsmanship and artistry he was supreme.

Preaching was the passion of his life, and he gave himself to it with a dedication that knew no reserve. It was the one thing on which he concentrated with an undeviating purpose. He wrote and re-wrote his sermons until they satisfied his fastidious sense of style. The study of words was one of his hobbies. He told once of how Henry Ward Beecher used to carry a handful of precious stones—diamonds, rubies, amethysts—in his pocket so that at odd moments he could let the sunshine play upon them and watch the varying lights flash from their facets. "I do it too," said Jowett, "only with words instead of stones."

In his Yale Lectures on Preaching he said: "Pay sacred heed to the ministry of style. A well-ordered, well-shaped sentence, carrying a body and weight of truth, will strangely influence even the uncultured hearer." He went on this assumption himself, polishing his language to the last degree, taking time and pains in finding the apt and telling phrase.

In his earlier ministry he was noted for the wealth and beauty of his illustrations; he was lavish to prodigality in his use of imagery. But later on, and particularly after his return from America, he pruned his style in this respect. The lily work on the top of the pillars was not so apparent. In the use of his voice he showed perfect management. It could not be called exclusively elocutionary, but it was as admirable an adaptation of means to an end as could well be imagined.

Jowett preached the sermon at the recognition of R. J. Campbell as minister of the City Temple, on the words, "Unto me, who am less than the least of all saints, is this grace given, that I should preach among the Gentiles the unsearchable riches of Christ," and it was said that "if anyone ever forgot the text it was not the preacher's fault. Again and again he declaimed it, exhausting every shade of meaning by broad or subtle changes of that voice of his. Then he murmured 'Unto me, who am less than the least'—tremulous, regretful, anguished—followed by 'was the grace given' in triumphant, virile, thunderous accents that crashed upon one with the uncompromising impact of a blow in the face. Dr. Jowett said many fine and memorable things that day, but what remained with one was the wonder of a voice that could open up the Scriptures by nothing more than varying inflexions and intonations. There was a recital of Paul's catalogue of unmentionable sinners, and then the sudden, quick, exultant pride, startling as a near shot, 'And such were some of you!' There was the threefold repetition of 'the sorrow,' the voice soaring higher and higher till it merged into actual song in whose ecstasy the very word 'sorrow' was transmuted into pure joy. These inspirations falling upon a receptive atmosphere opened a deep door into the preacher's personality. They had nothing in common with an elocutionist's trick. They were the expression of Apostolic triumph in the unsearchable riches of grace made vocal, the irresponsible trills of a soaring bird intoxicated with the blue in which it floats. Finer vocal efforts even than these may have been heard; it was what lay behind them that burned its way to the deeps of the soul."

Jowett did not spend time arguing in the pulpit; he proclaimed his message. And if he concentrated all his powers on preaching it could also be said that he almost concentrated all his preaching on the theme of grace. "There is no word," he once declared, "I have wrestled so much with as grace. It is just like expressing a great American forest by a word. No phrase can express the meaning of grace. Grace is more than mercy. It is more than tender mercy. It is more than a multitude of tender mercies. Grace is more than love. It is more than innocent love. Grace is holy love, but it is holy love in spontaneous movement going out in eager quest toward the unholy and the unlovely that by the ministry of its own sacrifice it might redeem the unholy and the unlovely into its own strength and beauty. The grace of God is holy love on the move to thee and me, and the like of thee and me. It is God unmerited, undeserved, going out towards the children of men, that He might win them into the glory and brightness of His own likeness."

This was what gave to Jowett's preaching the wooing note which was so often cited as one of its chief characteristics.

August 6, 1938

XV

Principal JAMES MORISON

IN hearing Principal James Morison I remember thinking how unusual an experience it was to have the privilege of listening to one who was the founder of a denomination which had come to have a recognised place in the religious life of the land.

On the base of the monument erected in memory of James Morison in Glasgow Necropolis is the inscription:

"Separated from the Secession Church in 1841 for testifying that Jesus died for the sins of all men without distinction or exception, he was spared to see his views of divine truth almost universally accepted in his native land. His ministry, begun under much obloquy, was finished amid the love and esteem of all classes of his fellow-countrymen."

This summarises the facts of Morison's career. At the outset it was turbulent; before the end all was peace. The man who had been regarded as a heretic came to be one of the most honoured and trusted theologians of his time. At the celebration of his ministerial jubilee the speakers included the most distinguished son of the Secession then living, the revered Dr. John Cairns. And one of the striking events of his later years was when he received a testimonial signed by 1946 influential laymen and ministers in Glasgow U.P. Presbytery, representing the Church of his fathers, from which, to his grief, he had been separated.

The Evangelical Union, which Morison was instrumental in founding when he was suspended from the ministry of the Secession Church, owed so much to him that its members were at one time almost as often known as Morisonians as E.U.s. And encyclopædias include Morisonianism as one of the sects of Scotland.

As a denomination the Evangelical Union was characterised from the very first by its evangelical spirit and its zeal in the cause of temperance. It continued under its original name until 1896, when it united with Scottish Congregationalism. It did not sink either its identity or its distinctive principles. The Congregational Union of Scotland is always officially described as "comprising the Evangelical Union and the Congregational Union as existing at 1896."

Rev.
W. J. DAWSON

Dr. T.
DE WITT TALMAGE

Photo:
ELLIOTT & FRY, London

Dr. GEORGE
MACDONALD

Photo:
ELLIOTT & FRY, London

Rev. HUGH
PRICE HUGHES

Photo:
TURNER & DRINKWATER,
Hull

The former E.U. Churches still retain several of their particular traits and some of the forms of the Presbyterianism from which they sprang. Many of the leading figures in the Congregational Union have been E.U.s. So it cannot be said that the denomination founded by James Morison has ceased to be a living force in the religious life of Scotland.

But it is not with Morison in that respect that I am here specially concerned. Nor is it with his fame and influence as a theologian, great as these were by reason of the expository works and commontaries of lasting value which came from his pen. My concern for the moment is with Morison as a preacher. It was as a preacher that he first revealed his power, and he remained a preacher of peculiar influence to the last.

During his first ministry in Clerk's Lane Church, Kilmarnock, it was impossible to find accommodation for the crowds anxious to hear him. On Monday evenings when he expounded St. John's Gospel the attendance was so large as to overflow into the galleries, and the weekly classes for young men and women were remarkable in size and interest. As he went about on preaching tours there was often a great spiritual awakening. On one occasion when he was in an Ayrshire village there might have been seen "seven hundred people sitting or standing quite contentedly for nearly two hours under a heavy rain listening to the Gospel."

When he came to Dundas Street Church, Glasgow, of which he was the first minister, his preaching made the same wide appeal. Along with his ministry he combined the Principalship of the Theological Hall, and the influence he exerted was one of the most notable in the life of Glasgow at that period. His preaching Sunday by Sunday and his week-night lectures made a profound impression.

In response to a requisition from ministers and office-bearers, Morison agreed to give a series of eleven lectures on the ninth chapter of the Epistle to the Romans, and East Regent Street Congregational Chapel, which was capable of holding 1500 people, was crowded to overflowing by men and women of all classes and of all ages. One evening, when he had spoken from eight to ten o'clock, he paused to remark that what remained of his lecture would take another hour to deliver, and if there were any who required to leave before the close, they could do so while the verse of a Psalm was sung. Though many had long distances to travel home, not one retired until the close of the lecture. In response to the urgent request of his hearers, he published the lectures under the title of "An Exposition of the Ninth Chapter of Paul's Epistle to the Romans," and a new edition was called for 40 years later.

One hearer of that period has told of how he came 30 miles to Glasgow every Saturday for the purpose of hearing two of its famous preachers on the Sundays. The two preachers were Norman Macleod, in the Barony, and James Morison, at Dundas Street. By Morison, he said, he was "edified, electrified, and awed." One Sunday afternoon he heard him preach on the words, "Say ye not, A confederacy, to all them to whom this people shall say A confederacy: neither fear ye their fear, nor be afraid." Speaking of this sermon, he said that to hear Morison "describe the futile attempts of men to bolster up the wrong, and to oppose the Governor of the Universe, and the accumulated woes which would come upon the transgressors, led one to think it was the crack of doom."

Yet there was nothing of the popular preacher about Morison, and anyone less like the founder of a denomination could not well have been imagined. The power he exercised was quiet and persuasive. By the time I heard him he had reached a serene old age, and I remember chiefly what seemed a strange combination of apparent austerity and reserve, along with the simple charm of a gentle and consecrated personality.

Early in his Glasgow ministry he suffered an injury to his vocal chords which handicapped him as a speaker for the rest of his life. At the beginning of a service his voice was so low and hoarse that it was difficult to hear him. Once "the larynx became heated," as he himself described it, the hoarseness was not so pronounced, but his voice never regained its clearly modulated tone. What triumphs he gained as a preacher and speaker were in spite of, rather than because of, his voice.

His preaching revealed perhaps as perfect a combination of the expository and the evangelical as we have ever had. It seemed as impossible for him to refrain from expounding the shades of meaning in a text or the general significance of a passage as to restrain himself from extolling the love of Christ. His manner was so quiet, his language so choice, and his style so lucid as to weave a spell over his hearers.

One who studied under Morison and knew him well has said: "He did not favour the idea of taking a text as a motto. His great purpose was to find out the mind of the Spirit in the words of Scripture and exhibit it. Often he said to his students and others that it was a small matter to the people what they thought on any subject, but it was of unutterable moment that they should know what Jesus thought. He urged them to let this be a never-absent guide in the preparation of their discourses, and the guiding he gave to others he followed from first to last himself. One result of this was that his preaching was a continual magnifying of Christ. Rare in scholarship, profound in thoughtfulness, fertile in illustration, and felicitous in expression, he was also intensely evangelical. He literally gloried in exalting the Saviour. To him Jesus was a kind of possession and the setting of Him forth in His love and might an unfailing joy."

The truth of an Atonement for all was James Morison's great theme all his life, and it is not surprising that his favourite hymn was:

> In the cross of Christ I glory
> Towering o'er the rocks of time;
> All the light of sacred story
> Gathers round its head sublime.

Principal A. M. Fairbairn, who was one of his students, said that to him "the greatest of all Dr. Morison's services had been the way in which his life had illustrated the high ideal of the scholar who never forgot that he was a Christian, and of the Christian who never forgot that he was a scholar."

September 3, 1939

XVI

Rev. C. SILVESTER HORNE

SILVESTER HORNE was essentially English, but he was an Arts student at Glasgow University, and nearly five years of his early manhood were spent in that city. It was in the undergraduate life at Gilmorehill that he first revealed some of the gifts by which he became famous in later life. In the students' societies he discovered his own power of public speech, particularly his skill in debate, and he became a leader among his fellows by his radiant personality and infectious enthusiasm. In the "Dialectic" he was a frequent and popular speaker, especially in the political contests, sharing the honours with several who became widely known, including Cosmo Lang, afterwards Archbishop of Canterbury; George H. Morrison, afterwards minister of Wellington Church, Glasgow; and Hugh Black, who became colleague of Dr. Alexander Whyte, in St. George's, Edinburgh, and later Professor in Union Theological Seminary, New York. He attended Elgin Place Congregational Church under the ministry of Dr. Albert Goodrich, but much of his time on Sundays was given to preaching in churches in Coatbridge, Airdrie, and the surrounding district, while he addressed many meetings of the Glasgow Foundry Boys' Religious Society. Many years afterwards he returned as preacher at Glasgow University, when he was specially thanked by Principal John Caird and Lord Kelvin at the close of the service. In the evening he spoke to 4,000 people in St. Andrew's Hall, and said he thoroughly enjoyed the environment.

There were two periods in the public life of Silvester Horne, and they were as different from each other as could possibly be. The first was when he was minister of the fashionable West End church at Kensington, London; the second when he was Superintendent of Whitefield's Central Mission and a Member of Parliament. In his Kensington days he gave a flawless example of pulpit propriety—with the perfect poise and the graceful gesture and the voice so modulated as to express every shade of emotion. One was caught, it was said, in the mingled spell of romantic chivalry and spiritual purity, hearing the music of delicate phrasing, feeling the grace of suggestive imagery and rejoicing in thought that was shot through with golden threads of insight, beauty, and emotion.

Then came the great change when Horne felt he could no longer be chained within the limits of conventional Church life, and he went forth to lead a great crusade at Whitefield's Tabernacle to reach the teeming thousands outside. His style inevitably changed. He adopted more and more the rough and ready methods of the public platform, and his voice lost something of its sweetness as it became frayed with incessant speaking. But his preaching passion burned brighter than ever. Instead of beautiful sermons he gave the people direct, intensely personal, and practical preaching transfigured by his own transparent sincerity.

To come into personal contact with Silvester Horne, I felt, was to receive a benediction. He was utterly unspoiled by success and fame; he took you to his heart at once, and the mingling of gaiety and high seriousness left an indelible impression. Winsome is the only word to describe his personality. Like Henry Drummond, he was every inch a gracious gentleman with a subtle but very real personal charm which was a veritable gift of God.

No platform speaker could excel Silvester Horne at his best. He had all the arts of the born orator. Grasping his coat lapels as he began quietly, he gradually gathered momentum until the sparks were flying and the whole atmosphere became electric. With shafts of humour, pungent phrases, and the glow of a burning passion, he could rouse an audience to an enthusiasm which brought them to their feet time and again. On some of these occasions he rose to passages of matchless eloquence. Never was there a finer example of one

. . . . . *attired*
In sudden brightness like a man inspired.

But there was another side to the man. The Boanerges of the public platform could be a singularly persuasive preacher in the pulpit. Tender as a woman and with the glow of his own personal experience, he could present the claims of the Gospel with wonderful power. It was said that he could give an evangelistic address of such directness and appeal as would have warmed the heart of Mr. Moody.

One sermon of his stands out in my memory. It was on the Parable of the Good Samaritan, and it was charged with all the sympathy and fervour of his personality. But what I remember best, and shall never forget, was a personal experience of which he told us. It had happened just shortly after his ordination to his

first charge when there fell to him the sad duty of breaking the
news to a young lady member of the congregation that her fiancé
had been drowned as the result of a boating accident.   He pictured how he went along to the house but could not summon up
courage to ring the bell.   So he paced up and down the street,
and as he did so he kept asking himself what all the books of theology
he had read, and all the training he had received in the Divinity
Hall, could do for him in a crisis of his life when he was faced with
a tragedy like that.   It was only after the struggle in his own soul
was over that he was able to do what was required of him.   No
one who heard Silvester Horne describe that occasion with all its
pathos, its heart-searching, and its grappling with a great mystery
could fail to remember the impression it produced.

What Silvester Horne never learned to do was to husband the
taper.   He spent his strength so freely that he literally burned
himself out when he was only 49.   One can still recall the wave of
emotion which swept this country when the news came from
Canada of his startlingly sudden death as he was walking with his
wife on the deck of a vessel entering Toronto harbour.   He went
quickly in one speechless moment.

> As a guest that may not stay
> Long and sad farewells to say,
> Glides with smiling face away,
>
> Of the sweetness and the zest
> Of thy happy life possessed,
> Thou didst leave us at thy best.

But he did a greater work and left a more abiding influence than
can be measured by any span of years.   I can never forget Silvester
Horne.   As Dr. Albert Peel has said, "He lived a chivalrous,
glorious, and knightly life; we shall not see his like again."

October 16, 1937

XVII

Dr. T. DE WITT TALMAGE

DR. TALMAGE was not by any means the greatest of American preachers, but it would be difficult to deny that he was one of the most popular. In this country, as well as his own, his constituency by means of his sermons published weekly was far larger than that of any of his contemporaries.

It would be easy to adopt the attitude of some who sought to dismiss Talmage as a master of volubility rather than of oratory, and to describe him as a pulpit mountebank. But if that had been all there was about him he could never have secured and held his vast audiences throughout the world. For many years there was not a city and hardly a township in America which did not print his weekly sermon in at least one of its papers. In this country they were published regularly in three religious journals—one of them with a very large circulation. Some years before his death it was estimated that his sermons were appearing in between two and three thousand papers weekly, and reaching approximately twenty-five million readers.

A graduate of the University of New York, Talmage held several ministries, and when he was still a young man he attracted great crowds to his church in Philadelphia. His success there brought him numerous calls from Chicago, San Francisco, and other cities, but he declined them all until he went to Brooklyn, where he was destined to do his greatest work.

When he began his ministry in Brooklyn, Henry Ward Beecher was at the height of his fame and Theodore L. Cuyler and other preachers of note had large followings. But in a short time Talmage's name was in every mouth. A great Tabernacle was soon built for him and still hundreds, and sometimes even thousands, of people were turned away. When the Tabernacle was burned down he preached for two years in the Academy of Music, and the number who failed to get in was said to be so great as to lead people to believe that the service was over and the congregation dispersing. Other two Tabernacles were built and also destroyed by fire. The contributions for the building of these three Tabernacles came from all parts of the world; when the last one passed away the congregation dissolved.

As a boy I heard Talmage's sermons read and discussed week after week, as they were at that time in many a home. Then I had the opportunity of hearing him on one of his last visits to this country. No church could accommodate the crowd, and the largest hall in the city was packed to overflowing. With fervent and dramatic power, he poured forth his torrent of oratory, piling up adjectives, heaping metaphor on metaphor, using a big brush to paint glowing word-pictures in vivid colours, now declaiming with tremendous vigour and next moment, on a tender note, touching deep chords of emotion.

His style can best be shown by an extract. Take this from his sermon, "An Easter Surprise," based on the text John 20. 6, 7: "The first lesson that I get from this subject is that truth and right-eousness cannot be successfully buried. This was not the first nor the last instance in which the world had tried to put truth and righteousness out of sight. But there is no rock so strong, there is no sword so sharp, that it can finally hinder the truth. Look now. It is Joseph in the pit. Look again. It is Joseph in the Court. Look now. It is Daniel in the den. Look again. It is Daniel in the Prime Minister's chair. Look now. It is the Covenanters crouching in the Highlands. Look again. It is the Free Church of Scotland. Look now. It is the 'Mayflower' putting into a stormy harbour. Look again. It is a continent of freemen. Look again. It is twelve Apostles laughed at in Jerusalem. Look again. It is a whole world receiving the Gospel. Look now. It is a bleeding corpse behind a sealed rock. Look again. It is a conquering Jesus, His foot on the fragments of a shattered grave. Let Truth, this daughter of God, be sealed; kindle around her the fires of Smithfield, or let her head drop off under the axe or the guillotine, or let her body in vengeance be torn limb from limb, then put her out of sight, bolt her into the grave with all the bolts of the prison-houses of earth, then roll against the door of the sepulchre all the boulders of the sea and all the granite of the cliffs, then let all the masonry that ever was forged guard that sepulchre; some morning early the earth will throb and the door will clang' open, and from the dust this daughter of God will arise, and go forth amid the wreck and ruin of the sepulchre to clap the cymbals of her triumph.

> "Truth crushed to earth will rise again,
> The eternal years of God are hers."

In a very characteristic Christmas sermon Talmage began thus: "How painfully and wearily one thousand years of the world's existence rolled along, and no Christ. Two thousand years, and no Christ. Three thousand years, and no Christ. Four thousand years, and no Christ. 'Give us a Christ,' had cried Assyrian, and Persian, and Chaldean, and Egyptian civilisations, but the lips of the earth and the lips of the sky made no answer.

"But the slow century, and the slow year, and the slow month, and the slow hour at last arrived. The world had had matins or concerts in the morning and vespers or concerts in the evening, but now it is to have a concert at midnight. The black window-shutters of night were thrown open, and some of the best singers of the world stood there, and, putting back the drapery of cloud, chanted a peace anthem, until all the echoes of hill and valley applauded and encored the hallelujah chorus."

After describing the scene in the stable, he went on to say:

"Let us open the door of the caravansary in Bethlehem and drive away the camels. Press on through the group of idlers and loungers. 'What, O Mary, no light?' 'No light,' she says, 'save that which comes through the door.' 'What, Mary, no food?' 'None,' she says, 'only that which is brought in the sack on the journey.' Let the Bethlehem woman who has come in here with kindly attentions put back the covering from the babe that we may look upon it. Look! Look! Uncover your head. Let us kneel. Let all voices be hushed. Son of Mary—Son of God! Child of a day—monarch of eternity! Omnipotence sheathed in that babe's arm. Omniscience strung in the optic nerve of that child's eye. That voice to be changed from the feeble plaint to a tone that shall wake the dead. Hosanna! Hosanna! Glory be to God that Jesus came from throne to manger, that we might rise from manger to throne, and that all the gates are open, and that the door of heaven that once swung this way to let Jesus out now swings the other way to let us in. Let all the bellmen of heaven lay hold of the rope and ring out the news: Behold, I bring you good tidings of great joy, which shall be to all people, for unto you is born this day in the city of David a Saviour which is Christ the Lord!"

A lawyer who went to hear Talmage regularly in Philadelphia said he had never heard him attempt to prove any proposition except once, when he adduced four passages of Scripture to prove that Christ died for sinners. The next day he said to him, "Dr. Talmage, are you going to change your style? You argued yesterday for the first time." Talmage replied: "I have not been very well, and had to fall back on an old essay that I wrote in the Theological Hall to be criticized by the professors. If you will excuse me this time, I promise you I will never do it again." And he never did. He did not bother his hearers with problems or seek to demonstrate any propositions.

Talmage was once asked a frank question: "To what do you attribute the cause that, while most preachers find it difficult to obtain a few readers or hearers, you count yours by millions?"

He paused for a moment and then he replied: "If I had to give one reason I think it would be this. In my sermons I always aim at helpfulness. Show me a congregation of five hundred people, I do not care where or when, and I will tell you how many of them want help. Every man to-day, no matter how successful he may appear, notwithstanding that his face is always smiling and the cheery word always on his lips, finds a craving for sympathy, strength and encouragement. You may take it that every man and every woman needs help. My one aim in preaching my sermons is to be helpful. I want to encourage every one of my hearers in the battle of life, to help them to get fresh strength for their conflict."

Modern thought never affected him, and he did not believe it affected his hearers. "The human heart," he said, "is essentially the same in all ages, and the same keys that drew music from it in the days of our fathers will strike responsive chords still."

Talmage had the ear of multitudes who were not in the least anxious about the results of Higher Criticism, to whom either Fundamentalism or Modernism mattered little, but who were concerned mainly with the struggle of everyday existence in a world where sin and sorrow darkened many of its days. Flamboyant his style might be, but he was able to lift the thoughts of the worn and weary folk who waited on his words to the thought of a brighter world to come.

"Confiding in the Lord Jesus Christ," he said, "death will be to you only the toilet-room in which you dress in immortal attire for glory. And now unto the God of all peace, who brought again from the dead our Lord Jesus Christ, that great Shepherd of the Sheep, through the blood of the everlasting covenant—to Him to be glory for ever and ever; and as the Psalmist broke down in his anthem of praise, and called on the stars, and the mountains, and the seas to play his accompaniment, so I break down under the glories of the anticipated resurrection morning, and I ask you to give your hearts to the Lord Jesus. If saved by Him now, you will, at the resurrection morning, join in the anthems of the redeemed, and for evermore dwell in the light of His glory."

January 28, 1939

XVIII

Rev. W. J. DAWSON

A NEW generation may have arisen that knows not W. J. Dawson. But the time was, and not so very long ago, when he had a great vogue, and his influence was potent and widespread, There are many of us who can never cease to be grateful for all that he meant to us in our early and impressionable years.

Perhaps it is as a literary mentor that he will be best remembered. Literature was his first love, and he was always more of the *litterateur* than the churchman. From his earliest days he was an insatiable reader, and no one suffered more keenly from the itch to write. Reading and writing were indeed the two passions of his life.

What a mass of material flowed from his pen. He was first of all a poet, and some of his lyrics are found in anthologies of modern poetry. In the realm of fiction he may not have been so successful, and none of his stories seems likely to live, whatever impression they may have made at the time they were published. It was in the sphere of literary criticism that he specially excelled. By his writings in the *Young Man* and in *Great Thoughts* he became the guide, philosopher, and friend of youthful readers everywhere, and his contributions, which were subsequently collected and published in his volumes on "The Makers of Modern English" and "The Makers of Modern Prose," exercised an influence which it would be almost impossible to overestimate in giving youthful readers a taste for the best literature.

Trained for the ministry of the Wesleyan Methodist Church, he served it at Wesley's Chapel, London, Glasgow and Southport, for 17 years. Then he became minister of Highbury Quadrant Congregational Church, London, where he continued until he left for America, and entered on the charge of the Old First Presbyterian Church, Newark, New Jersey. By that time he had a great reputation on both sides of the Atlantic, and his published works were having a wide circulation. Over twenty books came from his pen and he continued to lecture, particularly on literary subjects, all over the United States.

It was not until he came to Glasgow that W. J. Dawson became known as a preacher. There was something in the intellectual atmosphere of the city quite different from anything he had previously experienced. He found it bracing and exhilarating. It called forth the best that he had to give. If it is true that Glasgow discovered him, it is equally true to say that it was in Glasgow he first discovered himself as a preacher.

He confessed that he was a little puzzled at the rapid and extraordinary popularity he achieved almost from the beginning of his ministry in St. John's Methodist Church. But of the effect it had upon him he made no secret. "With what a thrilled heart," he said, "I went down to my church on Sunday evenings, knowing that I should find a crowd waiting at the doors long before the hour of service! How inspiring was the vision of that throng of faces turned toward mine, mostly young, all hushed and eager, waiting for the word."

Perhaps he was right in attributing a certain amount of his pulpit popularity to the changing conditions of the period. He had come to the city just when ideas were broadening out, and he proclaimed in public what had been passing through many minds. But a more definite attraction, especially for students and other young people, was his habit, which was something of a novelty at the time, of laying under contribution in his sermons the entire field of English literature. He would quote Shelley and Browning, William Blake, and Edward Fitzgerald. He saw, to quote his own words, "all religious and moral truth through the transfiguring haze of intellectual beauty."

None of the poets had a greater influence on W. J. Dawson than Browning, and Browning and Glasgow were associated in his memory by an unforgettable incident. "On a certain dreary day in December," he said, "I walked down Sauchiehall Street, and entered a book-shop for the purpose of buying an advance copy of Browning's last volume, 'Asolando.' Henry Drummond, the famous author of 'Natural Law in the Spiritual World,' was in the shop, and we talked a little of Browning and all that he meant to us. We came out into the rain-swept street together and suddenly stood transfixed, for on the other side of the street a newsvendor was displaying a placard announcing 'Death of Robert Browning.' As I read the fatal words the dreary street grew darker, as though all the tall, grim houses veiled themselves in crape. And, as I read, I thought the veils of crape on the dark houses became coloured banners, and on the dim air trumpets sounded, and up the dreary streets celestial convoys moved, stately, processional, triumphant."

It was not from popular audiences only that Dawson received encouragement during his time in Glasgow, where the length of his ministry was determined by the three years itinerary system of the Methodist Church. He was invited by Principal John Caird to preach at the University and he never forgot the kindness he received on that occasion from one who was himself the greatest preacher in Scotland. His outside engagements also included a service in St. Giles' Cathedral, Edinburgh, and he lectured all over the country. I am inclined to think he was greater on the platform than in the pulpit. Many of his lectures were on literary subjects, but I specially remember his great oration on Abraham Lincoln which held an audience of two thousand spellbound. It was indeed an oratorical *tour de force*.

One text of his I specially recall—"He called it Nehusthan" (a piece of brass). It was the type of sermon into which he was able to throw all the passion and dramatic power of which he was capable. That his hearers were roused to enthusiasm was not surprising. It was no uncommon thing for his Sunday evening congregations to break out into applause. At that time it seemed a strange breach of decorum in a people whose traditions of worship were staid and formal. Yet it was so deeply sincere that it seemed to suggest no element of irreverence.

On the other hand, when he had a different type of theme he could be intensely moving. In a sermon on the need for decision he awed his hearers with this final appeal: "You know what is right and wrong. It only remains therefore for me to press the question: *How long?* How long? For as these words reach you memories of the old home have stirred in you; the prayers of a long-dead mother have vibrated on the ear, and her dying voice has thrilled you; and you have thought of the men you have known, the lost men, all whose brilliant promise has burned into dead ash, and whose bright young lives have been blighted in an early grave. The way of transgressors is hard. How long halt ye between two opinions? *How long?* For the time is short. Nearer than we know stands the cloaked shadow, the inexorable messenger; and the year will soon dawn which will shine upon our graves.

> *Our life is a dream,*
> *Our time as a stream*
> *Glides swiftly away,*
> *And the fugitive moment refuses to stay.*

How long haltest thou between two opinions? *How long?* For life and death hang on the decision. Like a gay ship the young life bounds over the bright waters, and the silver voice of riot fills the sunlight, and 'all goes merry as a marriage bell.' But even now the tempest lowers; the sea shivers into foam as the wind strikes it; and the grey waves run in thunder, and break no more in ripples. Infirm of purpose, how long haltest thou between two opinions? Knowest thou not that he who steers no course steers the wrong course, that he who makes no decision has made the wrong decision? Dost thou not see, far away, yet ever nearer, that belt of white foam spanned by the thundercloud, smitten by the lightning, that last harbour, the final shore of doom? There is no time for delay; is Jesus with thee in the little ship? The storm comes on apace, and death is near; is He who stills the waters with thee now? Now is the time; there is no other. Claim the hour; the reversion of to-morrow is assured to none of us. I warn you, I appeal to you, I beseech you, but I cannot save you. You must choose; you only can. Remember the words of a great writer recently in our midst:

> *This passing moment is an edifice*
> *Which the Omnipotent cannot rebuild,*

and now, while it is called to-day, choose whom you will serve. Who this day will consecrate himself to the Lord?"

Rhetorical, some may say, and not the kind of thing to which we are now accustomed. But W. J. Dawson was a born orator, and his language suited his delivery. The oratorical style is dying out, but it came naturally to him. To have heard him when he was in full blast was indeed something to remember.

December 3, 1938

XIX

Dr. GEORGE MACDONALD

GEORGE MACDONALD, some may think, was more a novelist and a poet than a preacher. But even in his novels and his poems he was always preaching. And long after he had withdrawn from the ministry he continued to preach from the pulpits of many denominations.

His first pastorate was that of a little Congregational chapel in Arundel. Even then he was in delicate health, and some of his mystical sermons puzzled the simple-minded members of his church. After preaching for some time in Manchester, he became minister of a church in Bolton, and there he found a ready response to his message. The congregation was composed mostly of working men, who were greatly devoted to him, and were disconsolate when ill-health made it necessary for him to resign his ministry.

Thereafter he never held any settled charge, but he continued to preach whenever opportunity offered. Never, it has been said, was there a man who delighted more in preaching. Even when seated in the pew he was itching to be in the pulpit. To quote his own words: "Thoughts began to burn in me and words to come unbidden, till sometimes I had almost to restrain myself from rising in the pew where I was seated, ascending the pulpit stairs, and requesting the man who had nothing to say to walk down and allow me to take his place."

It was with the publication of his "David Elginbrod" that George Macdonald became famous. His verse:

> Here lie I, Martin Elginbrod,
> Hae mercy o' my soul, Lord God;
> As I wad do, were I Lord God,
> And ye were Martin Elginbrod

is well known, and has been often quoted as containing an epitome of his belief that God was not less merciful than man. In "David Elginbrod," "Alec Forbes," and "Robert Falconer," George Macdonald put all the force and power of his distinctive message.

"These novels," said Sir William Robertson Nicoll, "were sermons by a preacher who was almost consumed with the intensity of his message. They were fiercely positive in their preach-

ing that God is love, that God is Father. They denounced the
formulation of dogma. They were full of faith in the ultimate and
complete victory of the light. How wonderful it was to see the
young genius come forth to fight against the time-honoured dogmas
with his dazzling spear of youthful scorn and beautiful indignation!
The diamond point of his virgin weapons, the figure of the preacher
all glowing and poetic in a region of ultra prose—these were enough
to fascinate youth, and the heart was cold that did not fall in love
with his generous and tender dreams. The books were con-
structive. They were altogether noble in their tone and feeling.
No one could lay them down without thrilling to the thought that
truth and goodness and God are alone worth living for. Even
although it might be impossible to accept their full teaching, they
throbbed with a spiritual life which could not but communicate
itself."

For many years George Macdonald lectured all over the Kingdom on literary subjects, and I have a vivid recollection of his
lecture on Coleridge's "The Ancient Mariner." How he revelled
in his theme that night. It would be impossible to convey any
adequate idea of how he recited the verses :

> Day after day, day after day,
>   We stuck, nor breath, nor motion;
> As idle as a painted ship
>   Upon a painted ocean.
>
> Alone, alone, all, all alone,
>   Alone on a wide, wide sea,
> And never a saint took pity on
>   My soul in agony.

That was on a public platform, but I have an equally vivid
memory of him in the pulpit. He was then in his later years, and
with his white hair and long flowing beard he seemed a grand prophetic figure. What I recall most of all was his reading of the Old
Testament lesson beginning "Comfort ye, comfort ye my people,
saith your God." In his pure Scots accent, which residence in
England and on the Continent had never softened, he read that
great chapter with a wealth of sympathy and feeling which was
profoundly impressive. The very tones of his voice held the
crowded congregation in rapt attention and awed into a silence
that could be felt.

His preaching had by that time become less polemical than it
had been in his earlier years. It has been said that "in a sense it

Professor
JAMES MOFFATT

Photo:
VANDYK, London

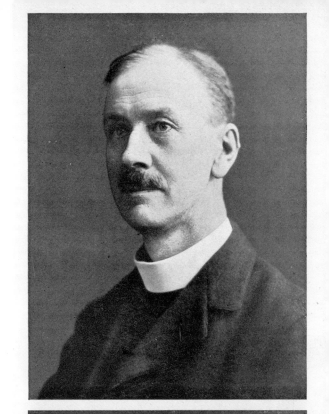

Dr.
AMBROSE SHEPHERD

Photo:

T. & R. ANNAN, Glasgow

To face page 80

RALPH CONNOR

Photo:
PIRIE MACDONALD

Dr.
ALEXANDER
SMELLIE

Photo:
J. P. MILNES, Stranraer

was true that he preached the love of God to a generation that needed that word, but as time went on and thoughts changed, he found his true sphere as a great prophet of immortality."

Heaven to George Macdonald was a home where there would be a glad reunion with loved ones who had gone before. Yet, even to this man of broad theology, heaven most of all was the place where "they shall see His face." It was this thought which inspired one of his most beautiful poems:

I fancy a twilight round me,
    And a wandering of the breeze,
With a hush in that high city,
    And a going in the trees.
But I know there will be no night there,
    No coming and going day;
For the holy face of the Father
    Will be perfect light alway.

I could do without the darkness,
    And better without the sun;
But oh, I should like a twilight,
    After the day was done!
Would He lay His hand on His forehead,
    On His hair as white as wool,
And shine one hour through His fingers
    Till the shadow had made me cool.

But the thought is very foolish;
    If that face I did but see,
All else would be forgotten—
    River, and twilight, and tree;
I should seek, I should care for nothing
    Beholding His countenance;
And fear only to lose one glimmer
    By one single sideway glance.

November 13, 1939

XX

Rev. HUGH PRICE HUGHES

IF ever there was a modern Wesley it was Hugh Price Hughes. He changed not only the outlook of Methodism, but even its atmosphere, and his influence on public life was profound and lasting.

Hughes played many parts in his time. He was preacher, lecturer, agitator, politician, reformer, editor. He made the West London Mission a great centre of social service, and the methods he introduced were taken as an example all over the country. His incursions in the political arena were not much to the liking of some who were otherwise his strong supporters, but that did not affect him in the least. He had an utter disregard of personal consequences; never was there a more fearless protagonist.

When Silvester Horne was a student at Glasgow University he wrote in a letter to his father: "To-day Hugh Price Hughes has been in Glasgow, and I have heard him twice—this morning at a Wesleyan church, and this evening in St. Andrew's Hall, on Total Abstinence. Both addresses were very characteristic—racy and telling. The sermon was just as much a platform speech as the evening lecture. He preached on witness-bearing. Speaking of the necessity for being bold in bearing witness, he said many ministers were afraid of Conferences or Unions, adding: 'Emancipation from the fear of the Wesleyan Conference is one of the most delightful things I know.'" This is an interesting early sidelight.

On the platform or in debate Hugh Price Hughes was a force of no ordinary kind. When he died *The Times* declared he was one of the six most popular speakers in England. He had every necessary gift—an extraordinary alertness of mind, a dexterous wit and keen sense of humour, a quickness and adroitness of repartee, and a personality electric and irresistible.

In journalism also he was a power to be reckoned with. Through the medium of the *Methodist Times*, which was founded for the dissemination of his progressive views on religious and public affairs, he moved and swayed opinion. By some of its venerable critics the paper was dubbed the Boy's Own Paper of Methodism,

while others jocularly declared it to be a very Hughesful publication. But it came to be admitted that "Price Hughes was a great
journalist endowed with an extraordinary flair for the right word
at the right moment, and an unusual gift of picturesque adjectives
which even the copious editor of *The Observer* might envy."

But when all else is said, there can be no question that Hugh
Price Hughes, first and last and all the time, was a preacher. Every-
thing was subservient to his passion for the proclamation of the
Gospel.

Here is a pen picture of him when he was at the height of his
power: "A dark-bearded man, lithe and muscular, with strong
chin, prominent jaw, flashing but humorous eyes, and strange
turned-up almost Mephistophelian eyebrows, dressed in the cor-
rectest of clerical garments, he hurled not thunderbolts but himself
at the audience. His voice was clear and of cutting quality, and
his direct and forcible words were stamped with the individuality
of an original and cultivated mind."

It would not be accurate to say that Hugh Price Hughes was a
great preacher. He might, perhaps, have been so if he had cared.
When his wife was once asked what she considered the greatest
triumph of his life, she replied that "it was his willingness not to be a
great preacher in the usual acceptance of that term. He had the
power to be one—the force and the intellectual equipment; but he
was willing not to be—to make himself of no account so that men
should hear not him, but Christ."

Thus it has been said that "had he been a greater preacher
he would never have done so much for the Church of Christ."

Hugh Price Hughes was at heart an evangelist. To his colleague, Mark Guy Pearse, he said: "You shall edify the saints, I
will pursue the sinners." And pursue them he did, whatever their
rank or station. In a charge to candidates for ordination he once
said: "You are not teachers merely, you are advocates. Your jury
is the congregation. According to the nature of the jury you will
present your case. Only remember you are there to win a verdict
for Christ." He himself was always preaching for such a verdict.

When he was in the throes of a great appeal and under the sway
of a strong overmastering passion for souls he was apt to forget
himself in some hasty impetuous words. I can recall such an
occasion. It was on one of his visits to Scotland and he was preaching to a huge audience which crowded a public hall. In the midst
of his moving final appeal some one in the gallery rose and made for
the exit. Hughes turned suddenly in his direction and shouted:

"Sit down, young man, sit down. If your mother were dying in the next street she would urge you not to leave at this moment."

It seemed an unfortunate impulsive outburst, but the preacher was terribly in earnest, and quivering with apprehension lest the impression which had been produced should be suddenly dissipated. He had been known to plead for a quarter of an hour with his own congregation: "Now, now, submit to Christ," but it was more than pleading: it was a demand that submission should be made there and then. "So," one of his contemporaries has said, "he stands in my memory, a man modern to the finger-tips, but none the less a mystic and an evangelist crying out to England, 'Submit to Christ'."

He died at the early age of 55. The end came swiftly and suddenly. He had never learned to take care of himself but lived up to and beyond his strength. Then it was found that "the enthusiasm that burned like lava had suddenly gone out—for earth and time."

W. T. Stead, a close friend with whom he had much in common, once described Hughes as "A Day of Judgment in breeches." And it has been said that he drove Parnell out of British politics and delayed Irish Home Rule for thirty years, Mr. Gladstone accepting his declaration that "what is morally wrong cannot be politically right."

But he is mainly remembered to-day as he himself would have wished, not as a force in public affairs, so much as a vehement, powerful preacher of the Gospel of Christ.

August 24, 1940

XXI

Dr. AMBROSE SHEPHERD

DR. AMBROSE SHEPHERD was unquestionably, in his own day and generation, one of the most popular preachers in Glasgow. During his ministry of sixteen years—from 1898 to 1914—in Elgin Place Congregational Church he drew the people as with a magnet.

His Sunday evening services in particular were attended by overflowing congregations. Queues were to be seen along two streets waiting for the opening of the doors; inside the church every available inch of accommodation, including the steps of the pulpit stairs, was utilised; and even then it was often necessary to turn many away. This continued year after year, so it could not be called any mere flash in the pan.

It was a remarkable record, and it was not secured by any adventitious means. Ambrose Shepherd had very definite natural gifts, but he never relied on them. He worked hard, and he deserved every bit of the success that came to him.

His son has said: "My father's sermons were composed with minute attention to verbal accuracy, that delicate sense of rhythm, which characterizes the work of an essayist. Each word with him definitely signified something, and he preferred one word to two. He would search for just that one word which exactly hit his shade of meaning, nor could he be satisfied with any substitute. He had an acute sense of words; they were to him like colours to an artist, materials out of which he must extract his absolute meaning. He had, too, that most priceless of literary gifts, a capacity for phrase-making, for striking out in relief some two or three words into a memorable phrase."

Dr. George H. Morrison, himself one of Glasgow's most popular preachers, once wrote: "If ever genius has been shown in dogged work, it was so in the case of Dr. Shepherd. If any young minister who reads these lines should conceive of preaching as an easy business—should think to shake a sermon from his sleeve, or to extract one from the inane, on Saturday—I only wish he had seen what I have seen, I only wish he had known what I have known, of the superb laboriousness of our friend. I had the good fortune

to be trained among hard workers both in the home and in the
Church; I have endeavoured to be worthy of that heritage; but
among all my friends I cannot think of one who has toiled so mag-
nificently as Dr. Shepherd that his people might have the finest of
the wheat. He did not take up his sermon at set hours. He
lived with his sermon all the week. When it was stubborn, he
fought with it, as Paul fought with the wild beasts at Ephesus. The
one thing he never did was to treat his pulpit carelessly. It was
ever his anguish and his crown."

This gives some impression of the toil that is necessary in order
to attain success in the art of popular preaching which some are
always so ready to depreciate. Ambrose Shepherd was under no
illusions in that respect. He made no apology for being a popular
preacher. He bent all his energies to become one, and he succeeded pre-eminently.

In declining to despise and depreciate popular preaching he
was in good company. Dr. Dale, in his closing years, greatly
deplored that he had been so afraid of making his preaching popular.
There were few men whose gifts were more scholarly and less
popular than Dr. Marcus Dods, but he never ceased to express
regret at the irrational prejudice against popular preaching and the
lasting ill-effects which this prejudice had produced on the Presbyterian pulpit in Scotland. Dr. Dods said that, in his college
years, if a man had much thought he was honoured, but if he knew
how to express it effectively he was regarded as shallow. And
Dr. Alexander Whyte powerfully warned young preachers against
a pseudo-intellectuality which leads to the despisal of popular
preaching.

But if Shepherd's preaching was popular, because he had studied
how to reach his hearers by the presentation of his message, had
striven to find the fit and telling phrase, and to develop an attract-
iveness and force of style which would capture the interest of his
hearers, that was not all. He would have agreed with Archbishop
Magee that there were three classes of sermons: Sermons you cannot
listen to, sermons you can listen to, and sermons you cannot help
listening to. His aim was to make his sermons such that people
could not help listening to them. But that was only the first
thing. He was anxious to make his sermons effective and helpful.
For mere rhetoric he had no use. If he aimed to be popular, he
aimed no less to be practical.

What, then, was his type of preaching? His own experience
had given him a knowledge of the problems of thought and life

which confront men and women day by day, and he set himself to deal with them frankly, fearlessly, in language which all could understand, and always to throw upon them the light that comes from Christ and His cross. He was, in the best sense of the term, an Evangelical preacher. It has been said that "what he began by preaching, what he continued preaching, and what he died preaching was a message of good tidings," the good tidings of Christ and Him crucified as the only hope of a weary and perplexed and sin-burdened world.

His Evangelicalism was not of a narrow type but something virile and bracing. This was what made his ministry so markedly a ministry to young people. His influence over them was one of the joys of his life. Preaching one day in Elgin Place Church, he said : "The first time I stood in this pulpit, the thought passed through my mind, 'What a centre this should be for young people!' And when I became the minister of this church I determined, God helping me, to bend my efforts in the direction of my first impression. In prayer and intention, I dedicated a large portion of my public ministration to the young men and women who might come within the reach of my words. And amid the things left undone, or which might have been better done, there have yet been some things to the good. I am constantly having letters, many of them from far-off places, written by young men whom, to the best of my knowledge, I have never seen, telling me that, because of words they have heard in this place of worship, they are trying to be what they know I would have them be, for God's sake, for their own sake, and for the sake of others."

Shepherd had little outward equipment as a speaker; it was by the sheer power of his preaching that he prevailed. His voice was thin and weak, and those listening to him for the first time began to wonder if ever he would be able to make himself heard. By and by, however, he had his hearers so completely under his sway that, in the intense stillness, even his whisper became audible, while the passion in his utterance had a greater thrill than that of any mere oratory.

Two of the secrets of his domination as a preacher were his living message and his profound personal conviction. Then, perhaps above all else, was the personality of the man himself, which was the driving dynamic behind all his words. "With him," it has been well said, "it was always the man, and not only what he said, that came home to his hearers. It was this, quite as much as his message, which held those vast audiences spellbound beneath his voice Sunday after Sunday for so many years. It was this that brought them to stand outside in the wet on wintry evenings, to be packed like sardines in the uncomfortable pews, to breathe the hot atmosphere of a great concourse; it was this—the pull of the man, the fire, the force, the magnetism of the man.

"And they were never brought forth in vain. Into every sentence, into every phrase, into every word, had gone the man's whole soul, the utmost concentration of his energies and resources. It was no facile utterance of mere fluency that they listened to, no 'gift of the gab' turned on like a tap for their temporary refreshment; it was to the man's best, to the choicest treasures of his genius and experience; to work with which he had wrestled, over which he had sweated; to work which (often as not) had stolen his sleep from him and taken his appetite away; to work upon which he had concentrated, and which now, with all the straight force of his conviction, with all the telling power of his few distinctive gestures, he spoke forth in their hearing. What he believed to be true he spoke forth; and to grace and adorn his message he prodigally expended all the gifts with which nature had endowed him. His pulpit was a sort of altar on which, week by week, he offered up to his vocation in the persons of his hearers the sacrifice of himself."

Ambrose Shepherd died at the age of 63, when he seemed still at the height of his power and influence. But in one of his sermons he said, "I, for one, have no more fervent desire than so to tire myself out in my day's work for God, and for man, that when I sleep I shall sleep well; and, for the rest, I know that I shall be satisfied when I awake in His likeness."

August 27, 1938

XXII

Professor JAMES MOFFATT

WHEN I went to hear Professor James Moffatt on a Sunday evening I had no thought of writing anything about the service. But I felt impelled to set down some general impressions.

The congregation itself made an interesting study. I am afraid the members of the church were completely swamped by the number of strangers. Specially noticeable was the large proportion of ministers—many of them in clericals, others in mufti. It would have been quite easy to form a quorum of a Presbytery or a Synod. There were some Glasgow ministers present who are "half-day preachers" during August, for we have "half-day preachers" as well as "half-day hearers." But the majority of the ministers seemed to be from elsewhere—many of them possibly visitors on holiday in the district.

It was not surprising that preachers should flock to hear Professor Moffatt, whose name is known throughout the whole English-speaking world, and to whom so many of them are indebted indirectly if not directly. He has been rather irrelevantly, if not even irreverently, described as "the man who wrote a new Bible." But his translation of the New Testament is now in common use, and church-goers are well accustomed to ministers reading or quoting from "Moffatt's Version."

How amazing have been Professor Moffatt's versatility and industry! It has been said that he reads theology by day and general literature by night, and is writing all the time. His published works have been in many different fields, ranging from learned volumes of exposition to a popular detective thriller. He has even been known to have devised cross-word puzzles. He turns from one sphere to another with apparent ease, taking everything in his stride.

It was once said of Robertson Nicoll that he edited five papers with his right hand and contributed to as many more with his left, that he was not a man but an army of men, directed by one cool controlling brain. Something of the same could be said of Professor Moffatt. He might almost be an army of men. How he does it all no one knows.

> For still they gazed, and still the wonder grew,
> That one small head could carry all he knew.

Professor A. J. Gossip tells the following: "Long ago now, Alexander Whyte was making a memorable speech at the jubilee of his friend, George Reith, and introduced a telling quotation 'from some minor character in Dickens, who it was, I forget.' And then, his eyes falling upon him in the audience, he added: 'Oh, there's James Moffatt. Who was it, Jim?' Whereat Moffatt at once gave text and context. Later, quoting 'The perseverance of the saints consists of ever new beginnings,' Whyte added: 'A favourite of mine, which I have always credited to So-and-So, yet one of my most learned friends assures me that is wrong. Who did say it, Moffatt?' And back came the answer: 'You are right, sir,' with the place at which to find it. So did this man carry about with him an uncanny mass of wide and accurate knowledge. And yet," adds Professor Gossip, "while every one thinks of Moffatt as the scholar that he was, the main thing in his life was not learning, but religion."

Although it is more than a quarter of a century since Professor Moffatt left the pulpit for a professorship, he has never given up preaching. When he was still in his native city of Glasgow he responded freely to requests for his services, and during his holiday from New York he is giving up many of his Sundays to fulfil preaching engagements.

Few scholars of eminence carry their weight of learning so lightly as he, and in the pulpit he makes an immediate impression by the simplicity and naturalness of his style. One never feels that he is straining after effect. It cannot be said that he has the orator's voice nor does he show the orator's sense of the value of light and shade in the tones of his utterance. What he has to say he says rapidly and animatedly, and his manner is always more that of the teacher than of a speaker eager to make a popular appeal.

It was interesting to find him reading the New Testament lesson, Matthew 7. 21-29, from the Authorised Version and not from "Moffatt's." But I noticed that, later on, in course of his sermon, when he was quoting from the passage in Matthew, he used the words of his own translation of the 27th verse: "The rain came down, the floods rose, the winds blew and beat upon that house, and down it fell—with a mighty crash."

The text of the sermon (which he always began with the same phrase, running it into a single word, 'the-text-of-the-sermon-this-evening) was Psalm 85. 8: "I will hear what God the Lord will speak: for He will speak peace unto His people, and to His saints: but let them not turn again to folly." He dealt specially with the last clause, and he had some pertinent things to say about the danger of turning to the folly of speaking too much. If we listen to God and stop talking for a bit, that leads to the right kind of action. When Jesus called Simon Peter and Andrew, they straightway left their nets and followed Him. They acted instead of speaking. It was the same with Matthew—he arose and followed Him. And when the vision came to Paul he did not stop to argue nor did he go to a religious conference to discuss his experience! He conferred not with flesh and blood.

For a long time there was not a single illustration from literature, notwithstanding Professor Moffatt's matchless store of such material. Then there came words contained in a letter from Carlyle to Emerson and a saying of George Meredith that "sentimentalism is enjoyment without obligation"—two unhackneyed quotations which aptly served their purpose.

Some years ago Professor Moffatt published a volume of his sermons under the title of "His Gifts and Promises." In a review of that work a writer said : "There is nowhere any parade of learning. The instructed reader discerns the scholarship in the background, but it is never obtruded. The preacher's aim is always directed toward the mark of unfolding what is in his text in such a way as to engage his hearers' minds and win their hearts by his message. Appropriately for such a purpose, the style is a model of simplicity and directness. It is indeed good conversation. Dr. Moffatt talks to his hearers with winsome charm and persuasiveness. That, with the subdued evangelical warmth which pervades the whole, makes the volume a fine example of interesting and effective present-day preaching."

And that is exactly what one feels after hearing Professor Moffatt in the pulpit.

August 20, 1938

XXIII

RALPH CONNOR

THE death last Sunday night of the Rev. Dr. Charles W. Gordon, of Winnipeg, better known under his pen-name of "Ralph Connor," has revived old memories and has set me the task of recalling an interview I had with him a good many years ago. He was taking part in the meetings in this country of the Pan-Presbyterian Alliance, and I remember some of his pulpit and platform appearances. Wherever he spoke there were crowded pews and earnest listeners. People who had been moved to laughter and tears as they read his pages, and had been lifted to higher conceptions of life and duty by his writings, listened eagerly to his words and yielded irresistibly to the fascination of his personality. But most of all do I remember the friendly talk I had with him, in course of which he spoke frankly of how he had been led to take up literary work and of the aim he always had in view.

By that time he had become famous as a Scots-Canadian preacher-novelist, and the name of "Ralph Connor" was familiar everywhere. His first book, "Black Rock," and his second, "The Sky Pilot," met with an immediate success in Canada and the United States, and that success was repeated in this country. They had the benefit of an introduction in Britain from Sir George Adam Smith. "I think," said Sir George, "I have met 'Ralph Connor.' Indeed, I am sure I have—once in a canoe on the Red River, once on the Assiniboine, and twice or thrice on the prairies to the West. That was not the name he gave me, but if I am right, it covers one of the most honest and genial of the strong characters that are fighting the devil and doing good work for men all over the world." Other books came in quick succession—"The Man from Glengarry," "The Prospector," etc., and "Ralph Connor's" influence had steadily widened.

Famous as he had then become, I found him to be at close quarters quite unassuming, with a singular charm and kindliness of manner. He was once described as having "a physique so slender as to be like a delicate stem from which the chandelier that crowns it sheds its unwearied glow." His physique was certainly slender, but he was bright, alert and vivacious, with all the zest in life of his iron "Sky Pilot." We found a common bond of interest in a reference to a Canadian journalist and religious leader known to us both, and the conversation never flagged.

Here is something of the story of his life as then told me by himself. He spent five years in Home Mission work in Western Canada amid scenes familiar to readers of his books. At a meeting of a church committee he gave an account of his work, which led Dr. J. A. Macdonald, then editor of the *Toronto Globe,* to ask for a sketch of Home Mission activities among the lumbermen in the Rocky Mountains for a new religious journal, *The Westminster,* which he was about to start. Then followed a correspondence which recalls that which passed between Robertson Nicoll and "Ian Maclaren" when the latter was led to embark on his literary career.

A long article reached Dr. Macdonald, but his keen editorial eye saw it was not what was wanted, but that it had possibilities. He therefore returned it with hints for reconstruction, and suggesting that the materials should be worked into a story of two or three chapters. This plan was followed, and the thing grew to ten or twelve chapters, and at the end of the year they were revised and issued in volume form under the title of "Black Rock." The second volume, "The Sky Pilot," also appeared first in serial form in *The Westminster,* as did also "Glengarry Days."

The nom-de-plume of "Ralph Connor," by a strange chain of circumstances, was chosen by Dr. Macdonald. When the first chapter was about to be published he asked the writer under what name it should appear. Telegraphic communications passed between them, but there was some misunderstanding as to the meaning of one of the messages, and Dr. Gordon first saw the pen-name, "Ralph Connor," when he received the magazine with the opening chapter of his story.

Of his view on the relative value and importance of the two departments of his work he left one in no doubt.

"I take it from the tone of your books, Dr. Gordon, that you regard yourself as a preacher first and a novelist afterwards?"

"You bet, every time," was the characteristically Canadian reply.

At the same time he did not depreciate the great sphere of influence given him by his writings. "I feel," he said, "that I have something to say to the people which I can say to them in this way."

Every one of his readers would be ready to endorse this. As a novelist he was as emphatically a man with a message as any preacher

who ever entered a pulpit.   Yet his method in his novels was not
to preach at people.   He knew a more excellent way.   He brought
humour and pathos and the skill of a real artist to his task, and with
the sunshine of his pages and the bracing effect of his teaching he
provided a moral and spiritual tonic.

Opinions will differ as to the respective merits of "Ralph
Connor's" books, but he never did anything better than "Black
Rock" and "The Sky Pilot."   Of "Black Rock," Robertson Nicoll
said: "If a better temperance story has ever been written I do not
know it."   It is full of life and tears and laughter and exquisite
tenderness, and all the essence of good literature.

To many of us "The Sky Pilot" will always be among "Ralph
Connor's" books what "The Window in Thrums" is among J. M.
Barrie's.   It is a wonderful story of the people in valleys remote
and lonely, and also, in the author's own words, "the story of how
a man with vision beyond the waving sky-line came to them with
firm purpose to play the brother's part, and by sheer love of them,
and faith in them, win them to believe that life is priceless, and that
it is good to be a man."

"Ralph Connor" wrote of life from personal experience in
unusual spheres, of its joys and sorrows, its tragedy and its romance.
And his religion was not a thing of maudlin sentimentality, but
something noble, manly, and bracing.   He had, it was said, the gift
to write books that appeal to boys and women and strong men,
that reflect the glory of primeval nature in the freedom of the
mighty forests and the mystery of the rivers, and the glory of God
in the power of a Gospel preached by men and women who, in
personal character and daily life, have the signs of a true Apostleship.

November 26, 1938

XXIV

Dr. ALEXANDER SMELLIE

DR. ALEXANDER SMELLIE is remembered as a writer rather than as a preacher, and his books are among our devotional classics. Yet he was in very truth a great preacher, with what can only be called charm as well as power.

Born in an "Auld Licht" manse, Alexander Smellie resisted all inducements to leave the Original Secession Church. As a student in Arts at Edinburgh University he had among his contemporaries men like Lord Haldane, George Adam Smith, J. M. Barrie, and W. P. Paterson.

Principal W. M. Macgregor first made the acquaintance of Alexander Smellie when he went up as an undergraduate to Edinburgh. "The three or four years which parted us in age," he said, "were enough to secure for him a boy's half-envious admiration, for he possessed what many of us coveted, knowledge and the gifts of style, and a marked distinction of character which we who could not imitate could at least perceive. Even as a lad he exhibited the elevation and purity of nature which distinguished him throughout his life, and after almost fifty years of friendship I can testify that I never heard him say a word of anyone which was ungenerous or unworthy." He made so great an impression on his fellows by his shining gifts that they thought almost any career might be open to him. Yet he never wavered in his course.

Years later, when Dr. Alexander Whyte began to think of having a colleague in the historic pulpit of St. George's, Edinburgh, his thoughts turned to Dr. Smellie, but without avail.

The only time he yielded to outside inducements was when he was prevailed upon to go to London to become editor of the *Sunday School Chronicle*. His work in that capacity was a brilliant success, but in two years he gave it up, feeling an imperative call to return to the ministry, and because, to use his own phrase, he missed "oh, so badly, the pastoral care of a little flock." So he went to the small Secession Church at Thurso with a stipend little more than the pay of an unskilled working man, and he had to be called twice to Carluke before he would leave that charge in the far north.

With Carluke his name became indelibly associated, and it is not infrequently referred to as "the place where Dr. Smellie was minister." All the churches of all denominations were proud of him. His fame, as it spread throughout the world by the richness of his writings, shed a lustre on the community in which he lived. But what prevailed above all else was the quiet persuasive power of his personality. He was so modest, so humble, so sincere, that he became universally beloved. That he was a saint, said one of his contemporaries, none who ever met him could question.

It would not be too much to say that in Dr. Smellie we had one of the choice spirits of our time. Shy and diffident, he preferred to work quietly in the background. He never courted publicity, but rather shrank from it, yet he was not one of those who profess indifference to these things, and treat any appreciative reference to their work with a lofty disdain. His readiness in any acknowledgment was only in keeping with the singularly gracious personality of the man. His letters of appreciation were, like all his writings, full of originality, grace, and charm. They are among the things some of us will long cherish.

Dr. Smellie's devotional books and his monthly notes for the International Bible Reading Association, which he contributed for so many years, carried his name and fame far and wide. What gained for him the honorary degree of D.D. of Edinburgh University was his "Men of the Covenant," which is universally regarded as one of the best of all the books on the Covenanters. It was a subject after his own heart, but it was the London publisher, Mr. Andrew Melrose, afterwards one of his most intimate friends, who persuaded him to undertake the task.

When he was presented for the degree it was said of his "Men of the Covenant" that the book was "a fitting tribute to the leaders in a national movement which it is easy to glorify or caricature, but not easy to delineate without losing touch with historic truth or falling into a dry, unsympathetic realism." His other books, such as "In the Hour of Silence," "In the Secret Place," are acknowledged to be amongst our classics of devotion.

In all Dr. Smellie's writings, as also in his sermons, there was an incomparable felicity of language. It has been said that as the mud-puddles in the streets yield arcs of glittering drops when struck with a stick, so every theme, even the dullest, rose to his pen as a tribute to his grace. Few men in the pulpit or out of it could use the English language as he did. The apt choice of a word, the music of the phrase, the subtle beauty of the sentences,

Rev.
DONALD McINTOSH

Dr.
DONALD FRASER

Dr.
WALTER C. SMITH

Dr.
JOHN KER

wove a magic charm. Then there was his rich literary allusiveness. He seemed able to recall almost from any age or from any author something appropriate to his theme.

Dr. Smellie said of John Woolman that his journal "reflects, like a flawless mirror, the lineaments of the man." The same might be said of his own style. It reflected not only his love of the beautiful in nature and life and literature, but the spirit of a man who was once described as living constantly in the atmosphere of the 13th chapter of 1st Corinthians.

I heard one of the last, if not the very last sermon Dr. Smellie preached from any pulpit. It was in Mains Street Original Secession Church, Glasgow, on the occasion of the ministerial jubilee of his friend, Professor Robert Morton. There was a passage from that sermon in which he said: "The most authentic and delicate of living poets, Mr. de la Mare, stands lost in wonder before a wild rose in the hedge, and sees its roots stretching back to the modest beginning of things.

> *Very old are the woods;*
> *And the birds that break*
> *Out of the briar boughs*
> *When March winds wake,*
> *So old with their beauty are—*
> *O, no man knows*
> *Through what wild centuries*
> *Roves back the rose.*

"Aye," he continued, "and no man can compute through what long, long centuries the Saviourhood of Christ roves back. The promises of the ancient covenant, its ceremonies and institutions, its happenings of joy and sorrow, its seers and priests and holy men were so many fingerposts on the road to Him. The Old Testament serves a multitude of uses, and is dear to our hearts for a multitude of reasons, but this is its noblest work, that it enables us to understand more adequately and to love more warmly our New Testament Redeemer, Jesus Christ."

It was a characteristic passage. Dr. Smellie had a rich, mellow voice, a restrained but effective delivery. Above all, there was about his personality in the pulpit something so winsome and gracious as to hold his hearers as if under a spell.

XXV

Rev. DONALD McINTOSH

IN the death of the Rev. Donald McIntosh there has passed away a
striking figure of distinctive personality and gifts, whose memory
will long be cherished by all who shared his friendship or came
within the range of his influence.

If ever any man was entitled to say in the words of that
strange and stricken genius W. E. Henley,

In the fell clutch of circumstance
I have not winced nor cried aloud,

that man was Donald McIntosh. Overtaken by blindness as the
result of an accident during his college course he resolutely continued his studies and in due course qualified for the ministry.
What would have proved to most men a crushing calamity was to
him only an obstacle to be overcome. He triumphed over apparently insuperable difficulties. Nor did he seek the pity of any,
for he was always radiant in spirit, the victor and not the vanquished.

Seven years ago another devastating blow fell upon him when
he lost his devoted wife on whom he had come to lean so heavily.
To be deprived of her constant co-operation and invaluable help
seemed an irreparable loss, and it was feared by his friends that his
days of usefulness might be over. Again, however, his unconquerable soul triumphed over apparent defeat. Sorrowing, but
not as those who have no hope, he took up once more the burden
of life. In a succession of students, some of whom are now in the
ministry, and bearing the marks of his influence, he found guides
who led him about the city as he discharged his pulpit and pastoral
duties. And at home he had the companionship and inspiration of
his daughter, Miss Barbara Ross McIntosh, who has made a name for
herself as an author of poems and stories, her literary gifts triumph-
ing over her blindness and the physical infirmity which has cut her
off from the activities of life.

Ordained to the ministry of the Congregational Church in
Scotland, Mr. McIntosh held charges at Cruden Bay, Kilsyth,
Aberdeen, Coatbridge, and Nairn before his retirement in 1927.
But his retirement proved to be but the entry on a wider and even

more influential ministry than he had yet exercised. Since he came to Glasgow nine years ago he had been constantly engaged in "locum tenens" work in many of the leading churches of the city. In this capacity he served the Partick and Hillhead Congregational Churches, but all his other engagements were with congregations of the Church of Scotland, and it was impossible for him to respond to all the requests for his services. Particularly striking was his occupancy of the central pulpit of Renfield Street Church, where for over a year he attracted overflowing congregations. But it was the same wherever he went. Crowds flocked to his preaching, whether in the centre or the suburbs, the East end or the West end.

Of his possession of pre-eminent pulpit gifts there could be no question. While these gifts may have been largely natural, he did not fail to cultivate them assiduously. He took infinite pains with his pulpit preparation. His style was largely peculiar to himself. Some may have felt that he had a superabundance of purple patches and eloquent flowing periods, "balanced and pointed like sonnets," and, perhaps, rather frequent recourse to "apt alliteration's artful aid," while the torrential rush of his eloquence, like a river in spate, when the words came tumbling and tripping over each other, made it sometimes difficult for his hearers to follow him as clearly as they wished.

But it would have been impossible to think of Mr. McIntosh as other than he was. He could not take preaching easily. He was a man burdened with a message which had the note of conviction, of authority, of urgency. When he rose to impassioned force and fervour in his delivery and gave rein to his extraordinary vocabulary, there was the spectacle of a man on fire with his message.

His choice of subjects and titles sometimes called forth criticism. But it must be admitted that he had a flair for what would arrest and attract those who were quite impervious to the conventional method of appeal. And even when his title seemed sensational there was nothing sensational in his sermon. An ecclesiastic declared some years ago that whatever Mr. McIntosh's subject or its title, he never failed in his preaching to bring his hearers near to God and face to face with his claims and the offer of Jesus Christ. Mr. Asquith when Chancellor of the Exchequer, frequently heard Mr. McIntosh in his first church at Cruden Bay, and he remarked with real discernment—"That man is always preaching for a verdict." The remark remained true of his preaching to the last.

Transparent sincerity was an outstanding characteristic of Mr. McIntosh, both in the pulpit and out of it. The popular preacher is not always the painstaking pastor, but he was tireless in his performance of pastoral duty, and never more so than in the charges he served as "locum tenens."   He trudged many a weary mile and up many a long stair in seeking out the people committed to his care, or, for that matter, in trying to help even those who had no claim upon him.   Interested in everything that interested his fellows (he followed eagerly the football results), he soon found common ground for conversation.   And in homes darkened by sorrow his presence carried comfort, for the man who was a Boanerges in the pulpit had another side to his nature.   While it was by grim, dogged determination and an inflexible will that he was able to overcome his heavy handicap and make his way in life, he possessed along with these qualities of granitic strength a tender and sympathetic heart.   And as pathos and humour usually go hand in hand, it was not surprising that he had a keen sense of the humorous aspect of things.   He had a connoisseur's delight in stories, and he could tell them with the skill of a born raconteur.

True and loyal to the core, Mr. McIntosh stood by his friends in fair weather and in foul, through good report and evil report, grappling them to his soul with hoops of steel.

But he cannot be grudged his rest and his reward.   Through his last illness he bore himself with that calm serenity of faith which sustained him all his days, and he silently preached from his deathbed as eloquent a sermon as he ever thundered from a pulpit.   Now he has seen the day break and the shadows flee away.   His eyes, long blind to the sights of life, have opened to a more glorious vision.

He passed away early to-day, and thus there came true in his own experience the lines to which he often referred:

> *Night slipped to dawn and pain merged into beauty,*
> *Bright grew the path his eager feet had trod;*
> *He gave his salutation to the morning,*
> *And found himself before the face of God.*

It would be impossible to think of that eager, questing, intrepid soul as being inactive even now.   There must be other ministries for him in other spheres.

June 26, 1937

XXVI

Dr. DONALD FRASER

THE first time I met Donald Fraser was when he came home as a young missionary from Livingstonia on one of his earliest furloughs. The last time I met him was just shortly before his final illness. On the first occasion I heard him thrill a Sunday School with one of his famous "lion stories" which became so well known later on. On the last occasion, as we sat in his room at the Church Offices, he talked intimately of some of his future plans and projects—never, alas! to be entered upon. Between the two there stretched a period of many long years—crowded years for him of work abroad and at home, and the young missionary had become a famous figure. But he was still the same Donald Fraser, with the winning smile, the kindly voice, the charming manner.

And now he has gone, and his life and labours on earth are at an end. The facts of his career have already been fully recorded, and it is not my intention to repeat them. I wish rather to give some general and personal impressions. Of his abiding place in the history of missions there can be no doubt. He would have been the last to claim that he was a great explorer like David Livingstone, or a missionary statesman like Robert Laws. But he accomplished a work peculiarly his own which no one else, perhaps, could have done.

The mission station which he founded at Loudoun, in Central Africa, is as fine a memorial as any man could desire, and no missionary of his generation did so much to awaken missionary interest in the churches at home. That in itself was a notable achievement. As a popular advocate of missions, he has had few equals. While he was not a born orator of dramatic impassioned power, he had unusual gifts of eloquence, at once vivid, winsome, and compelling. And there was always "that caress in his voice that won a thousand audiences, both in Livingstonia and at home."

Of his experience in more recent years, one almost hesitates to write. Yet, in justice, something must be said. It was no secret throughout the Church that he was often worried and wearied with it all. He never grudged work; he was even too eager for it, but uncongenial official relationships chafed his spirit and clouded his sky. Time and again he longed to be back in Africa among those who knew him best and where no shadow ever existed. He never was, and never could be, an ecclesiastic. I remember him once saying that he was a child in regard to matters of form and procedure, but many would love him none the less for that.

If his life has left a lesson, so also have his last illness and death. As he lay in the nursing home his thoughts seemed to be continually of others. He was always thinking of those in distress—his char-woman's daughter who was ill, people whom he knew to be in trouble, those who had gone through the same operation—and many were the kindly messages that were sent at his request.

The resignation of some young missionaries who had not been long in the field was much in his mind, and one day he remarked: "I wish one could get them to think of Mr. Courtnald, who was buried for six months in his ice hut, but stood it all out of his devotion to the interests of science. If he could do that, could not missionaries come through more than that out of devotion to their Master?"

The nurses were greatly touched by his gracious courtesy and his warm appreciation of the slightest service they were able to render him. When he was able he was interested to hear about those who had been inquiring for him, and he was filled with grati-tude. On learning that the inquirers included some one who was on the dole he was deeply moved. "The dear man," he said, "how kind of him."

While the end came suddenly, it was not without a struggle. But in his suffering he spoke of how his mind had been "running tremendously on the wounds of Christ, wounded for our trans-gressions, bruised for our iniquities." He was conscious to the last, and passed away in peace.

A death so triumphant may well preach as impressive and telling a sermon as any he ever preached in his lifetime. It was entirely in keeping with the spirit of praise that was ever in his heart during his last days that the request was made for "no mourning," and that the note of the funeral service in Wellington Church was one of thanksgiving. This prompted the inclusion of the hymn:

> *All creatures of our God and King,*
> *Lift up your voice and with us sing*
> *Alleluia, Alleluia.*

And there was a peculiar appropriateness in the verse:

> *And thou most kind and gentle death,*
> *Waiting to hush our latest breath,*
> *O praise Him, Alleluia!*
> *Thou leadest home the child of God,*
> *And Christ our Lord the way hath trod.*

The Paraphrase with which the service closed had also a special significance. On the morning of the Sunday on which Dr. Fraser died he lay listening to the church bells, and as the curtains were drawn and the sunshine streamed in at the window, he began softly to repeat:

> *Blest morning whose first dawning rays*
> *Beheld the Son of God,*
> *Arise triumphant from the grave*
> *And leave His dark abode.*

At the close there came not the "Dead March," but the "Hallelujah Chorus," in which he used to exult when he went regularly at the New Year in Glasgow to hear "The Messiah." It was with its note of victory pealing forth that the service ended.

The body was afterwards cremated, and the family hope that the ashes will eventually be taken out and buried in the kindly soil of his adopted land "among his own folk" in Africa. There could surely be nothing more fitting. It is not as an organising secretary he would wish to be remembered, nor even as Moderator of Assembly, but just as Donald Fraser of Livingstonia.

> *To lift the sombre fringes of the Night,*
> *To open lands long darkened to the Light,*
> *To heal grim wounds, to give the blind their sight,*
> *Right mightily wrought he.*

August 26, 1933

XXVII

Dr. WALTER C. SMITH

WHEN the Church of Scotland had Dr. George Matheson as its poet-preacher, the Free Church of that period also had a poet-preacher in Dr. Walter C. Smith. We have each of them represented by two of their hymns in the Revised Church Hymnary, and while Matheson's "O Love that wilt not let me go" stands supreme in fame and universal popularity, one of Smith's is steadily coming into favour in our church services as a glorious song of praise. It is the hymn beginning:

> Immortal, invisible, God only wise,
> In light inaccessible hid from our eyes,
> Most blessed, most glorious, the Ancient of Days,
> Almighty, victorious, Thy great Name we praise.

Coming from Orwell, Dr. Smith spent 14 years in Glasgow as minister of the Tron Free Church before he went to the Free High, Edinburgh, with which his name was to be specially associated.

Orwell, on the shores of Loch Leven, gave Walter C. Smith the pen-name under which his first long poem was published, and it is the theme of some of his haunting verses, as when he wrote:

> Hark! how the skylarks sing,
> Far up about God's own feet,
> And the click of the loom is in each little room
> Of the long bare village street.
>
> Yonder the old home stands,
> With the little grey kirk behind;
> There are children at play on the sunny brae,
> And the shouts come down the wind.
>
> Ah me! for the shore and the lake,
> Where the small wave ripples and frets!
> The land has its weeds, and the lake has its reeds,
> And the heart has its vain regrets.

It was during his ministry in Glasgow that Dr. Smith published "Olrig Grange," which many consider one of the greatest of all his poetic works. It brought him wider fame than he had yet achieved, and it moved that great theologian, Dr. R. W. Dale, of Birmingham, to write the only article which a book of poetry ever brought from his pen.

In the High Church, Edinburgh, Walter C. Smith rose to the height of his influence as a preacher. He was a contemporary of Dr. Alexander Whyte, of St. George's, and he had his own following among the students. J. M. Barrie, in "An Edinburgh Eleven," has said: "During the four winters another and I were in Edinburgh we never entered any but Free Churches. Even our Free Kirks were limited to two—St. George's and the Free High. After all, we must have been liberally-minded beyond most of our fellows, for, as a rule, those who frequented one of these churches shook their heads at the others. To contrast the two leading Free Church ministers in Edinburgh as they struck a student would be to become a boy again. The one is always ready to go on fire, and the other is sometimes at hand with a jug of cold water. Dr. Smith counts a hundred before he starts, whilst the minister of St. George's is off at once at a gallop and would always arrive first at his destination if he had not sometimes to turn back. Dr. Whyte judges you as you are at the moment; Dr. Smith sees what you will be like to-morrow."

In the Tron Church, Glasgow, Dr. Smith had attracted a great congregation, and during his long ministry in the Free High, Edinburgh, his hearers included many of the leading men of the day. Professor John Stuart Blackie was one of those who delighted in his preaching. On the occasion of Dr. Smith's ministerial jubilee, Sir George Adam Smith said: "It was a great ministry he achieved in Glasgow and Edinburgh. For over thirty years his preaching was one of the strongest spiritual forces among the educated men of both these cities. It was Biblical and expository; it was ethical, and with strong insight into human nature; it was carefully prepared, and of a high and simple style, with great beauty of illustration. But its chief quality was a strenuous and solemn engagement to win men and women from the world and from themselves for Christ; an anxiety, sustained from first to last, to feed the flock committed to his charge, and to guide their characters through the perils of the time, which no man better understood or more faithfully presented than he."

It is not difficult for anyone who ever heard Dr. Smith to recall the impression he produced. It is difficult, however, to describe it. There was nothing tempestuous in his style, and he was a master of eloquence rather than of oratory. In the pulpit he was a handsome and distinguished-looking figure. He had a rich, flexible voice and a fine natural ease of manner and style. But what one best remembers is the light in his eye capable of expressing many things, and the power of personality which lay behind all his preaching.

It has to be admitted that many of the prolific writings of Walter C. Smith cannot be ranked as great poetry. At the same time it is equally true that he wrote some poems of real genius which can never be forgotten. He could describe with humour and pathos and quaint kindly satire certain types of character in which were reposed the insincerities, religious and scientific, of the period in which he lived. But a critic well said that to make no mention of the religious element in his poetry would be a conspicuous example of presenting the play of "Hamlet" with the omission of the Prince of Denmark. He had a special sympathy with those who were perplexed in thought, and since he had himself won through to a sure faith he was able to help others out of his own experience, as when he wrote:

> I love the kirk, with ages hoar,
> I love old ways, but Christ far more;
> I love the fold, I love the flock,
> But more my Shepherd and my Rock
> And the great Book of grace
> That mirrors His dear face.

After being at one time suspect in certain quarters, Dr. Smith won his way to the confidence and esteem of all classes, and he lived to receive the honour of being Moderator of the General Assembly of his Church. Other distinctions came to him, but perhaps none he would have valued more than to live in the lives of those he influenced.

J. M. Barrie has told of meeting an Irishman in London "who talked with such obvious knowledge of Dr. Smith's teaching, and with such affection for the man, that by and by we were surprised to hear that he had never heard him preach nor read a line of his works. He explained that he knew intimately two men who looked upon their Sundays in the Free High, and still more upon their private talks with the minister, as the turning-point in their lives. They were such fine fellows, and they were so sure that they owed their development to Dr. Smith, that to know the followers was to know something of the master."

It was a tribute any preacher or teacher would covet.

February 11, 1939

XXVIII

Dr. JOHN KER

A MONG my earliest memories I recall hearing Henry Ward Beecher on what must have been his last visit from America. I was too young to have any real understanding of what he said, but to this day I remember the tones of his voice as clear and melodious as the pealing of a silver bell. Of John Ker, whom I also heard in those early years, impressions have remained which have enabled me in later life to appreciate more fully his remarkable gifts.

John Ker, like his contemporary, John Cairns, was one of the great figures of the old U.P. Church which, in the days of its separate existence, made so notable a contribution to religious life and thought in Scotland, and was in itself so rich in men of outstanding gifts and power. In what was really a galaxy of talent John Ker shone with a brilliance all his own.

In his published works he left a legacy which is still of high value to-day. His "Thoughts for Heart and Life," "The Psalms in History and Biography," "The History of Preaching," and his "Letters" continue to yield fruit to every discerning reader. But it was by his two volumes of sermons that he won enduring fame.

The first volume soon made a profound impression everywhere. Dean Alford declared it to be the best volume of sermons in the English language; it was said that no book was more frequently seen on the tables of undergraduates of Oxford and Cambridge; and that it was more widely read than the work of any other preacher except Frederick Robertson, of Brighton. The book went through fourteen editions during its author's lifetime. And it has been said that "whoever opens that volume of sermons, even after many years, will be aware at once of an aroma of exquisite things

> *Like fumes from fragrant treasures* . . .
> *In graven censer old,*

for he wove into the fabric of his Church's life a thread of beauty which has not been torn away, nor ever lost its hue."

While the sermons may be found to-day to lack certain qualities which distinguished those of John Henry Newman and Frederick Robertson, they have some "distinctive excellencies not found elsewhere, and are assured of a place that is their own in the higher literature of religion." They have also in them that which makes for permanence. There may be applied to these sermons a saying from one of them: "There are books and men that seem beyond others to have the power of aiding insight. All of us have felt the affinity of nature which makes them our best helpers; the kindred clay upon the eyes by which the Great Enlightener removes our blindness."

During his ever-memorable ministry in Sydney Place Church, Glasgow, Ker responded beyond the limits of his feeble strength to the claims of work outside the congregation. He became one of the most popular platform speakers in the city. It was quite customary for him to speak in public every night in the week, and he is said sometimes to have addressed five meetings in one evening. That is enough to prove that he was no recluse who, because of his seclusion from the turmoil of life, was able to produce pulpit work of such high and enduring quality. He preached three times every Sunday, and he was not remiss in pastoral work, for his name has been handed down from parents to children as that of a tender shepherd of souls.

But, first and foremost and all the time, he was a great preacher. He spoke in the pulpit without notes of any kind, but it has been said that "the language was so beautiful, so full of delicate fancy and fine feeling, that no mortal man could have so spoken if the choice of words had been left to the spur of the moment." As a matter of fact, all his sermons were carefully written and mastered before he went to the pulpit, yet his delivery had nothing of the nature of a recitation about it. He spoke with an air of the utmost ease and spontaneity. It struck his hearers as "a kind of extraordinarily elevated conversation."

He was fragile physically and somewhat deformed in appearance, but when he came to some of the more telling passages in his sermons his face became lighted up and transfigured with a rare beauty of its own and you beheld the triumph of the spiritual over the physical. With uplifted finger and trembling lip he would hold his hearers spellbound as, in low tones, he delivered his most tender appeals.

One can picture him in the following description by the late Dr. J. H. Leckie: "The written style of a preacher is, in its broad lines, generally conditioned by the fashion of his spoken address. Thus, the stately, sweeping periods of John Caird were suited to the uses of his voice—that magnificent organ whose rich and mani-

fold music follows us down the years.   And, in like manner, the
diction of Ker was admirably attuned to the character of his delivery,
which was clear, pleasing, melodious, and of varied modulation.
His periods were generally short, his paragraphs never cumbrous, or
such as might depend on the roll and surge of a powerful voice.

"He was sparing of gesture; but his rugged face was illumined as
he spoke by an inward brightness, as is a graven image when a lamp
is lighted within.   There was passion in his discourse, but it was
not of the kind that resembles a torrent of fire.   Rather was it like
a warm radiance shining through the windows of a home where
strong conviction and quiet faith dwell at peace with understanding and hope and acquaintance with grief.   He did not seek
to take the mind of an audience by violence or to carry it away on
an impetuous tide of words.   His way was rather to win his hearers,
taking them captive unawares, showing them the beauty of the
Gospel and the meaning of their lives, leading them by still waters.
While he avoided rhetoric, his language was rich in colour, but
the tones were constantly subdued.   While there were never any
purple patches there were many places where symbol and fancy
bloomed like flowers."

Some of his phrases were as haunting as they were illuminating.
He said that the prophets, in foretelling Christ, often "disappeared
in their theme, like the lark in the sunlight in which it sings."   His
idea of the future life as seeing the reconciliation of faith with
knowledge was: "A glorious temple where study and adoration
walk side by side, and angels who know clasp hands with angels
who burn."   The persistence of opportunity, so long as life endures,
was enforced in the phrase: "To be suffered to remain on God's
footstool is to be within reach of the steps of His throne."   Speaking
on the nature of Christ he said: "It was like the sea, which is so
mighty as to shake the earth, yet holds the most delicate flowers,
with all their filaments unbroken in its bosom."   Without faith in
the Father of Jesus Christ, he said, "the thousand eyes of the night
would glitter pitilessly on our misery, and its fixed cycles would be
coiled around us like chains of despair."

Such sayings may serve to illustrate, in part, the style of John
Ker's sermons, but there were other qualities which cannot be
illustrated: "their admitted strength of mental grasp, their dia-
lectical power and piercing analysis, their supreme gift of commend-
ing to mind and heart the sovereign religious ideas of God, Immortality, Incarnation, and Redemption in Jesus Christ."

October 15, 1938

XXIX

Professor ROBERT MORTON, D.D.

PROFESSOR ROBERT MORTON was without question one of the most distinctive as he was one of the most venerable personalities in the Church life not of Glasgow only, but of Scotland at large. He was as well known outside his own denomination as within it, and wherever he was known he was held in honour and esteem.

He was gradually recovering from illness, and was looking forward to his diamond jubilee celebrations. The arrangements for these were completed and had been submitted for his approval. It was hoped and expected he would be able to attend both the Presbytery dinner to be given in his honour and the congregational meeting. But it was not to be. He had spent Saturday evening in his study, but about nine o'clock he became suddenly ill, and in a very short time he died from heart failure. It was a swift passing, but few men could have been readier for the call whenever it might come.

Professor Morton was in many ways a remarkable man, and he had a wonderful career. His triumph over physical disability was enough in itself to make the story of his life something out of the ordinary. But his friends are anxious that the actual facts about the accident in his early life should be given. According to them, he never worked in a sawmill. What happened was that, as a boy, between eight and nine years of age, he was playing beside some machinery, in which he allowed his hands to be caught, with the result that both of them had to be amputated. The fact that, in spite of this, he fought his way through school and college to the ministry was no small tribute to his patient perseverance in overcoming difficulties. With his artificial hands he contrived to do many things, even writing letters, which some of us found easier to decipher than the letters of others with no such disability. To many he was known as "the minister with the black gloves," although they did not know all the tale of heroic endeavour that lay behind his constant wearing of these gloves in the pulpit as well as in the street.

It was my privilege to know Professor Morton over a period of years. I had many a talk with him—in his own home, on the street, and at public gatherings of all kinds. Busy man as he was, he would always stop in the street, not only to exchange greetings, but to discuss one or other of his many and varied interests. I was constantly struck by the shrewd discernment of his outlook and by his fine catholicity of spirit. Advancing age seemed only to increase his tolerance and his radiant optimism. He was generous in his appreciation of others, and it always gave him pleasure to direct one's attention to young men of promise who were worthy of being brought into notice.

It was difficult to keep pace with all Professor Morton's public activities, for he was deeply immersed in the philanthropic and charitable work of the city. And yet he was always first of all the Christian minister. Learned as he was and a competent man of affairs, we shall always think of him most of all for what he was in himself. That is only another way of saying that his greatest asset of all was his own personality. And what a personality it was—in its gentleness and quiet strength, in its unaffectedness, its transparent sincerity and real nobility. I was often struck by his resemblance to the late Principal John Cairns, of Edinburgh. And the resemblance was not in appearance only. Professor Morton may not have been gifted with the massive oratorical power of John Cairns, but he had something of his benign and simple greatness of personality.

As a preacher and speaker, Professor Morton, if not eloquent, was invariably impressive. He wasted no words in getting to the point of what he had to say; he attempted no flights of rhetoric, and indulged in no fireworks. Simply, lucidly, effectively he stated his case without artifice or trimming of any kind. But behind all he said—and this was particularly true of his preaching —there was felt all the charm and power of his winsome sincerity and earnestness.

In these days when ministers are apt to be accused in some quarters of a mercenary spirit, the example of Professor Morton deserves to be quoted. Talented as he was above the ordinary, he laboured to the end of his life for a humble financial return. He was less well off than a Church of Scotland minister on the minimum stipend, for he had no manse. But in his own Original Secession Church he had received every distinction it was in the power of his brethren to bestow, and in other Churches he was honoured and beloved. All denominations were proud to regard him as the "Grand Old Man" of the Glasgow ministry. Nor was he without the appreciation of the community generally. It is a satisfaction to-day to recall that on more than one occasion his fellow-citizens, as well as his fellow-Churchmen, gave vent to their feelings of veneration instead of waiting to tell the next generation how great a figure we had in our midst.

I remember at the celebration of his jubilee ten years ago Professor Morton said that to die was the last thing he intended to do, and that to the end of his days his congregation in Mains Street Church would have what strength and energy were his. So it has come about. Although in his 84th year, he continued, until his illness a month or two ago, to carry on without assistance all his pulpit and pastoral work. He has died, as doubtless he would have wished, while still minister of Mains Street Church. He was in harness to the very last, and had no waiting period of enforced inaction after his long life of incessant industry. It was for him a quick and easy transition from the activities of earth to the full-orbed energies of heaven.

> *Nothing is here for tears, nothing to wail,*
> *Or knock the breast: no weakness, no contempt,*
> *Dispraise or blame, nothing but well and fair,*
> *And what may quiet us in a death so noble.*

November 26, 1932

Photo: T. & R. ANNAN, Glasgow

To face page 112

XXX

Dr. JAMES HASTINGS

I HAVE no hesitation in including Dr. James Hastings in this series. He was himself a preacher of peculiar power, although he may have been better known as the friend and helper of other preachers by reason of the monumental works he published for their benefit. As an editor and encyclopædist he attained fame before his death, and no name in the generation to which he belonged is more likely to live than his.

I remember him telling me how he was first led to enter on that particular field of activity which he made so largely his own. He had been settled as minister at Kinneff of a small country congregation of farmers, crofters, and cottars, worshipping in a building that had long before seen its best days. In a short time he had secured the erection of a new church, and then he took the step which has been fraught with such far-reaching effects. "After I had visited all the congregation as often as it was reasonable to expect, I wondered," he said, "what I might do now. I might have begun gardening, but I was much more interested in books." So he decided to start a monthly theological magazine, and the *Expository Times* was born.

The story of the early days of that now well-known monthly is worthy of being told; it seems to savour of fiction rather than of actual fact. The young minister found a bookseller in a small way in Aberdeen who agreed to become the publisher, but Dr. Hastings undertook the entire financial responsibility on his stipend of £160! The first number came out; and Dr. Hastings had the second ready when he found that his publisher-bookseller was ill and absent from business, leaving the shop in charge of a little girl who should not have been away from school. Nothing daunted, the editor himself went behind the counter in the little shop, and for more than a fortnight he remained there and sold the *Expository Times* and any books the public wanted to buy, while the little girl looked in now and again to give him a nod of encouragement.

In a short time, however, the publication of the *Expository Times* was undertaken by the well-known Edinburgh firm of Messrs. T. & T. Clark, who have been responsible for it ever since. It soon made a place for itself, and came to be indispensable to its readers. Dr. Hastings wrote a great deal himself, and he stamped his personality on every page. It is a tribute to his editorial instinct and foresight that so many of the features of the magazine which he introduced at the beginning have proved so popular and useful that they have had to be continued right on to the present time.

But the *Expository Times* is not the only memorial of Dr. Hastings. His "Dictionary of the Bible", "Dictionary of Christ and the Gospels," "Dictionary of the Apostolic Church," and his "Great Texts" volumes all represent indefatigable industry and tireless research. Then there was his *magnum opus*, the "Encyclopædia of Religion and Ethics," in thirteen volumes. Professor Stalker once said that "the appearance of the Hastings Dictionaries has for the first time really done for the Church what Augustine felt the need of."

For 27 years Dr. Hastings continued in the ministry and he never allowed his literary interests to interfere with his pulpit and pastoral work. When he held a heavy city charge in Dundee he was able to overtake the visitation of his congregation by hiring a cab (it was before the days of motor-cars), thus saving both time and the physical strain of long tramps through city streets. There is a tradition of his being seen busy in the cab correcting proofs as he drove from one house to another. That would only have been characteristic of the man, for no one was ever more careful of odd moments. He wasted no time; he found rest in change of occupation; and he never threw away the scraps of leisure which most men highly value. It was this, along with his immense industry and pertinacious perseverance, that enabled him to overtake a mass of work which seemed beyond the capacity of any single individual.

When Dr. Hastings left Dundee and returned to a country charge at St. Cyrus, he repeated what he had done at Kinneff, and was again instrumental in securing the erection of a new church. A further proof of the devotion and success with which he applied himself to his ministerial work was found in the fact that at St. Cyrus, where the congregation itself was small, he had a Bible Class with a roll of sixty, and a considerable number—especially of the men—were present at every meeting.

It was certainly not because he was a "stickit minister" that Dr. Hastings ultimately resolved to devote his whole time to his literary undertakings. He was emphatically a success in the ministry, and even after he had no charge of his own he continued to give his services freely as a preacher. He was frequently called on for special occasions, and no minister in a difficulty ever appealed to him in vain.

In private Dr. Hastings had a gentle voice and manner, and this was equally characteristic of him in the pulpit. He was always perfectly natural. No manuscript was used. He had a rapid yet easy utterance, speaking freely out of his wealth of knowledge. While devoid of oratorical fire, his delivery was animated, and there was a warmth which soon communicated itself to an audience.

What he strove after was not eloquence or artistic adornment but the effective elucidation of his subject. He made no parade of learning; it was an education to see how this man with all his unrivalled background of knowledge could gain the ear of his hearers by preaching which had a beautiful simplicity and a lucidity which was the perfection of unstudied art. His sermons were strongly evangelical and closely applied to everyday life. To be able to preach a doctrinal sermon which was a bright and living thing, attractive and interesting even to the average hearer, and to be able to give it a point and warmth of appeal, is a rare gift, and that gift Dr. Hastings undoubtedly possessed in a singular degree. He could, if he cared, have spoken to scholars in the language of the schools—none could do it better when the occasion arose— but in the pulpit he took the more excellent way of addressing himself to men and women in the pews bearing the burdens of everyday life, and thus "the common people heard him gladly."

Dr. Hastings is said to have been the greatest servant of Biblical scholarship in his generation. He has left truly monumental works in his great Dictionaries and Encyclopædias. But he has also left the memory of a personality of rare nobility. One of his oldest friends said of him before his death: "We find Dr. Hastings now sitting among his lexicons with proud titles to his name, and with a great reputation. We find him with the whole Christian public recognising his work gratefully. But we find him still an unspoiled man, a man of humble faith, a man of brotherly kindness, a true, good man."

He died in 1922, but his influence lives on, not only in the works which bear his name but in the lives of those whose hearts are filled with affectionate gratitude at every remembrance of him. He was in the real sense of the term a great man, and he had the humility which is always associated with true greatness. His fame will endure not only because of what he did but because of what he was.

December 13, 1938

XXXI

Dr. R. F. HORTON

WHEN an American newspaper described Dr. R. F. Horton as
being "just what would have resulted if Matthew Arnold
had become a Salvation Army captain," it gave a graphic indication
of that blending of culture and evangelism of which Horton was one
of the most conspicuous examples. At Oxford, where he rose to
the coveted post of President of the Union, he was one of a brilliant
band of young men which included Lord Milner and several others
who became great public figures. His own inclination was towards
a purely academic career, although he also had hopes of proceeding
to the Bar.

Yet, even when he was at Oxford, it was said of him that "he
could no more resist the impulse to evangelistic work than an
artist can keep his hands off pencil and palette. If he was not
preaching he must be busy in the conversion of drunkards, or the
confirmation in the faith of Liberals and Nonconformists."

The parting of the ways came when he received a requisition
signed by 100 residents in Hampstead—one of whom was Mr.
Asquith—urging him to become the first minister of a new Congregational cause in that London suburb. At first he agreed to
carry on the work for a year without pledging himself further, but
finally he yielded to the persuasions of the people and settled down
to what proved to be his life work. It was his one and only charge:
never was the value of a long ministry more clearly demonstrated.

From the first, and to the end of his life, he scorned the use of
clerical garb in any shape or form. On his declaration, "I will
wear no clothes to distinguish me from my Christian brethren," he
was chaffed by Hugh Price Hughes, and was also made the subject
of an amusing and famous cartoon.

Horton was a man of ceaseless activity, and his influence was
felt in numerous ways. He was a voluminous author, a zealous
social worker, an enthusiast for Foreign Missions, a champion in
many a public cause, and he had the capacity of being able to inspire
others with something of his own ideals. First and last, however,
he was a preacher.

The wide appeal of his pulpit work was evidenced by the con-

Dr.
JAMES HASTINGS

Photo:
WM. CROOKS, Edinburgh

Dr.
R. F. HORTON

To face page 116

Dr.
ALEXANDER
GRIEVE

Rev.
A. E. WHITHAM

gregations flocking to his ministry.   All classes were represented
—men of letters, doctors, lawyers, rich men of business, and poor
people who scarcely knew where their next meal was to come from.
For every one he seemed to have a message.   His monthly lectures
to working men became as great a feature as Dr. Joseph Parker's
Thursday services in the City Temple.

It would not be inaccurate to say that Dr. Horton was a preacher
who was largely governed by his moods, although that does not
quite convey what is meant.   Tennyson said of Swinburne that he
was a "tube through which all things were blown into music."
Horton has been described as "a voice through which the emotions
of the soul issued in impromptu passion, now breathless with
adoration, now flaming with wrath. . . . He was the spiritual
impressionist.   He saw truth, as it were, by flashes of lightning,
where others arrived at it by the slow operation of intellect.   He
surrendered himself to the emotion, and soared with wings."

In the earlier years of his ministry he was once described as
"an artist in demeanour" and as a symbol of "carven rest," while his
preaching was said to be "all persuasion."   That was not true of
him in later life.   At times he could be as disquieting as a prophet of
wrath, although at others he could be as soothing as a strain of music.

His different types of preaching were once aptly delineated by
Mr. A. G. Gardiner.   "The preacher is in the grip of some strong
emotion which colours hymn and prayer and lesson, peeps out
from the little fable he addresses to the children, and is fully revealed in the sermon.   It is as though he has come from some
sudden vision of the world's wickedness and the world's wrong.
It is visible and audible.   He has seen the world thundering by
to destruction in a frenzy of luxury and pleasure and heedless riot.
He leans forward with outstretched hands, pleading, pleading.
He is torn with bitter agony.   His voice is shaken by the tumult
of his feelings.   A moment more and the tense bow must break.
But he draws himself up, closes the Bible, and the troubled sea sinks
down in the calm of a hymn and the peace of the benediction.

"Or perhaps it is a bright moment in spring.   The song of birds
is heard on the heath, and he has seen the snowdrops bursting from
their winter prison—the first syllables in the poetry of the year,
the heralds of the pageant of the earth.   And his heart sings with
the glad tidings of the new birth.   He has seen the finger of God
in the woodlands.   He has heard the voice of the eternal by the
seashore.   He has picked up a shell, and found in it thoughts that
do lie too deep for tears.   For the earth is filled with the whispers

of the Most High.   And, full of this sweet assurance, the service flows on golden wings to a golden close.

"But a day comes of bitter self-abasement.   He is bowed down with the sense of failure.   He is stricken with remorse, with the passion of weakness and futility.   A word, a breath, has set all the chords vibrating to the miserere.   The sorrow of the world is his, and the sin of the world too, for what has he done to alleviate the one and wash out the other?   He is the unfaithful servant.   He is the bringer of a message which he has failed to deliver.   The world is deaf because he has not unstopped its ears; the world is blind because he has not unsealed its eyes.   He stands, like Whittier, in the presence of his soul and arraigns it like a felon."

Nothing could better convey an idea of the changing emotions of this remarkable preacher, or the complete thrall in which he was held by his theme.   It was said that he rarely "enjoyed" preaching as ministers often do.   He came more and more to regard himself as a mouthpiece for a message with which his soul was burdened.   He did not argue in the pulpit, he proclaimed.   He strove to curb the oratory for which he had a natural gift, and to restrain the rhetoric of which he was a master, just as he sought to conceal his brilliant scholarship lest anything should dim his burning passion to declare the will of God as it had been revealed to him. Thus it has been said that at the close of a sermon his hearers, instead of wishing to rise and cheer or to express admiration of such an effort, felt that they should fall on their knees in prayer.

Horton's views on inspiration brought him into conflict with many earnest souls, and his leaning towards a liberal theology was an offence to others.   But he had a disinclination for controversy which grew stronger the longer he lived.   "My doctrinal views," he was wont to say, "are summed up in the words 'Jesus Christ'."   And having said that, he said all.

In practical affairs he was very much an "innocent abroad," but his sincerity was transparent.   On all who knew him he left the impression of a man who walked with God and had wholly surrendered his life to the Divine leading.   There was no divergence between his theory and his practice, his preaching and his living.

Christ's love he taught, and His Apostles twelve;
But first of all he followed them himself.

As Gibbon said of William Law, he "believed all that he professed and practised all that he enjoined."

November 4, 1938

XXXII

Rev. A. E. WHITHAM

SINCE his sudden death in his prime the Rev. A. E. Whitham
has become more widely known than he ever was in his lifetime.

His peculiar gifts were appreciated throughout the churches of
his own denomination, but two posthumous volumes, "The Dis-
cipline and Culture of the Spiritual Life" and "The Pastures of His
Presence," introduced him to a much wider public as a preacher
and teacher of quite unusual insight and power, and more than a
touch of genius.

During his itinerary as a Methodist minister Mr. Whitham spent
a term in Edinburgh, but that was not his only connection with
Scotland, for he married a Paisley lady. I heard him more than
once; it was also my privilege to have talked with him, and I have
clear memories of his sparkling brilliance. Whether in the pulpit
or on the platform, or in private conversation, he could not help
scintillating. It was as natural to him as breathing. Handsome
and distinguished in appearance, overflowing with wit and humour,
it is not too much to say that he was loved by all who knew him.

His daughter has said of him: "At an early age we, his daughters,
were thrilled by his joyous interest in everything, and our greatest
delight was to be with him, whether at a cricket match, or a sym-
phony concert, or just at home listening to him as he talked,
simply and naturally, about the religion and the fine flowers of
human culture which meant so much to him. He was the perfect
companion who made real life glow with the excitement of a fairy
story. He was truly a master in the art of living, and it was exhilarating to see him give himself fully and vigorously to that art.
His poise was remarkable; his catholicity of mind, his genius for
friendship, his patience with folk who tried him sorely, his unforgettable humour.

"It is difficult," she continues, "for me to give adequate expression to every one of the many facets of his nature, but remarks
from other people will help. One says: 'There was much about
him of the troubadour and more than a little of the Franciscan.
There was in him a beautiful blend of goodness and gaiety. He

was one of the gayest and most seriously religious persons I have ever met, and how he yearned to enter more deeply into the secret of the saints.'

"And now he has finished his work on earth. He has been taken suddenly, without warning, but he was quite ready. One of his last words to me—though we did not know it then—was: 'He has the hammer that can strike my bell.' It was to have been the subject of his last sermon on Christmas morning, but he was not well enough to give it. But that was the thought which shone in his mind at the last."

In the pulpit he might strike off aphorisms and epigrams with the utmost ease; he might be speaking at one time with all the dash and daring of youth, and then next moment be plumbing the deep things of the soul and the tragedies of human experience.

How graphically he could arrest attention at the outset. Here is one of his introductions: "Christianity began and ended with a cry—the cry of a child in a crib, the cry of a mature man on a Cross. What is more natural and homely than the one? What is more awesome and obscure than the other? How far removed is the lullaby of a mother soothing her restless child from that poignant groan, 'My God, my God, why hast Thou forsaken Me'?"

The following may be quoted as an example of how he could let his imagination soar: "On my return (from a visit to a museum) I must have dozed, for I thought I was treading the streets of the Holy City, pottering about like a tourist. In my wanderings I came upon the museum of that city of our dreams. I went in, and a courteous attendant conducted me round. There was some old armour there, much bruised with battle. Many things were conspicuous by their absence. I saw nothing of Alexander's nor of Napoleon's. There was no Pope's ring, nor even the ink-bottle that Luther is said to have thrown at the devil, nor Wesley's seal and keys, nor the first Minutes of Conference, nor the last (I was sorry about that, because my name was in it). I saw a widow's mite and the feather of a little bird. I saw some swaddling-clothes, a hammer and three nails, and a few thorns. I saw a bit of a fishing net and the broken oar of a boat. I saw a sponge that had once been dipped in vinegar, and a small piece of silver. But I cannot enumerate or describe all I felt. Whilst I was turning over a common drinking cup which had a very honourable place, I whispered to the attendant, 'Have you not got a towel and a basin among your collection?' 'No,' he answered, 'not here; you see they are in constant use.' Then I knew I was in Heaven, the Holy City,

and amid the redeemed society. 'Knowing that He came from
God and went to God . . . took a towel and basin.' "

Take this as an example of his power of illustration. He had
been preaching on the text: "Christ in you the hope of glory,
Whom we preach, warning every man and teaching every man in
all wisdom, that we may present every man perfect in Christ."

The sermon was a plea for a complete consecration, and he
concluded by telling of a horse that had never been in the shafts
before, and was writhing as the bit and bridle were fitted. Here
was his story. "A man grasped the reins. The lookers-on said
'He will kill you,' but the man replied, 'No, he won't. He will
feel the quiet of my hands down the reins into his mouth.' It is
Christlike to do that with people in this restless age, to live so,
in the peace of God, that men shall feel the quiet of you running
from your life into theirs."

Rev. W. Bardsley Brash has written: "A. E. Whitham preferred
the 'twopenny coloured' to the 'penny plain.' We have never
known a more colourful personality. He was modern and catholic,
and withal deeply evangelical. There was about him an infectious
gaiety and also a deep seriousness. . . . He was widely read, and
a man of marked literary gifts. He was paradoxical and yet central,
and had the gift of striking our spirits broad awake. He was
Chestertonian in his paradoxes, Shavian in his fierce exposure of
hypocrisies, and deeply mystical in his spiritual ardours. Many
could quote of him the words which he loved, 'He has the hammer
that can strike my bell'."

But nothing finer has been told of him than this: "He loved to
tell the story of the Curé of Ars, who asked a French peasant, who
came daily at noon in his blue smock frock from the field to medi-
tate in the church at Ars, what he thought and said as he knelt.
The peasant gave answer with the unforgettable words: 'Jesus
looks at me, and I look at Him.' A. E. Whitham had 'gazed and
gazed'—that is why his preaching helped so many to *see* the Lord."

August 19, 1939

XXXIII

Dr. ALEXANDER GRIEVE

IN the death of the Rev. Dr. Alexander Grieve, of Greyfriars' Church, Glasgow, we have lost no ordinary man. He was so unassuming and so unobtrusive, and he went about his work in life so modestly, that many perhaps never realized his true greatness. But those of us who were fortunate enough to have known him intimately were never deceived either as to his transcendent gifts or the inherent nobility of his personality.

The abilities of Dr. Grieve were of a remarkable order. He was a man of encyclopædic knowledge; nothing appeared either too great or too small for his grasp. He seemed to know something about everything. While he had the wide range, he had also the exact and specialized mind, and there were subjects on which he could speak with an authority which none could dispute. In theology he naturally excelled, but he was also an expert in languages—Scots, English, and foreign alike.

It may seem strange that such a man should have been left to spend practically the whole of his working life in charge of a church situated between the Candleriggs and George Street. Certainly it is one of the historic churches of the city, with a long roll of eminent ministers, but its circumstances and surroundings have greatly changed with the passing years. That Dr. Grieve should have maintained such a fine congregation in such a locality, and should have bound the members by such bonds that they continued to attend from all parts of the city, cannot be regarded as other than a great achievement. It proved his power alike as preacher and pastor. But how great was the cost?

Dr. Grieve revealed such brilliant promise as a student and gave evidence in his mature years of possessing such outstanding ability that it is not surprising there should be an idea he never quite came into his own. Few men were so completely equipped for a Professorship. Not only had he the necessary learning himself, but he had also rare skill in communicating it to others. He could make the most abstruse subject clear and sparkling. But with all his gifts he lacked that of "window-dressing." He was so humble and so retiring that in the race for position he was easily outclassed. Happily, his talents were helpfully employed from time to time when he stepped into the breach to conduct classes in Glasgow U.F. (now Trinity) College, and many students, both past and present, must have happy memories of his temporary occupancy of their Professor's Chair.

And even amid all the distractions of his heavy city charge, Dr. Grieve was able to make considerable contributions to literature. He has left behind him a biography of Willibrord, the Netherlands missionary, and a translation of Professor Deissmann's "Bible Studies."

What Dr. Grieve might have accomplished if his life had run along different grooves and he had enjoyed the leisure of a scholar's life we can only dimly guess. The wonder is that he was able to do so much in the way of literary work. And while we might have been inclined to grudge the time he spent, and the stairs he climbed, in his faithful pastoral visitation, it was by no means fruitless work. On hearts and lives which came under his personal influence he made an abiding impression. For Dr. Grieve had more than great gifts; he had also a rare personality. A scholar to the finger-tips, he was at the same time very human. He loved all the innocent things of life, and found delight in its simple pleasures. An angler from his youth up, he never lost his zest in the art, and a game of chess was a favourite relaxation. In all his relations with his fellows he revealed a big, generous, warm heart. Of few men could it be more truly said that

> *He nothing common did or mean.*

With no place for petty feelings in his nature it was little wonder that men were instinctively drawn to him.

And so to-day, notwithstanding all his intellectual powers, it is for the loss of Alexander Grieve, the man, that we mostly mourn. He was so true, so strong, and yet so tender, so noble in his spirit and his outlook, that his passing has meant a real impoverishment to many. And if, in the eyes of those who knew the things of which he was capable, he may never have come into his own in the way of preferments and appointments, these things never seemed to trouble him, just because he was so unconscious of his own greatness. His life was contented and happy and, in the highest sense, eminently successful. For surely no man ever captured more fully the trust, the love, and the affection of those who knew him. Compared with these, any mere passing honours would have counted but little with Alexander Grieve.

January 29, 1927.

XXXIV

Dr. JOHN KELMAN

DR. JOHN KELMAN was a prince of the pulpit who was laid aside from active duty and then cut off before what seemed, to human eyes, to be his time. Into his span of life, however, he had crowded more than many men who long outlived him.

Almost from the first he was a marked man. Dr. Alexander Whyte was anxious to secure him as his assistant as soon as he left the Divinity Hall. But Dr. Whyte, for once, was a day late. Kelman had just been engaged by George Adam Smith to be his assistant in Queen's Cross Church, Aberdeen. These two men were congenial spirits, with abounding vitality and gallant souls. George Adam Smith profoundly influenced his young assistant, broadening his interests, stimulating him to read and study and cultivate his style.

Then Kelman was called to Peterculter in Aberdeenshire, and in that country village he soon established a reputation of his own. It was not only his preaching that exerted an influence. His personality made a profound impression on all sorts and conditions of people. Not far off a crowd of navvies were engaged in work in connection with a water supply scheme. Kelman made friends with these men, and it used to be said that when a fight broke out in the navvies' camp, it was not the village policeman who was sent for but the minister. The personal power by which Kelman afterwards swayed more than one generation of Edinburgh students was first shown by his influence over that very different class of men.

Six years later he entered on what was perhaps the greatest time of his life. The New North Church, Edinburgh, when he became minister there in 1897, was far past its best days and in a situation for which there seemed to be no future. But soon there was a complete transformation. The church not only became crowded, but queues began to gather before both services. Young men and women were among his most numerous and most eager hearers. His Bible Class on Sunday evenings was equally popular. Students flocked to it in such numbers that it had to be transferred from the hall to the church.

Dr.
JOHN KELMAN

Dr.
D. M. McINTYRE

Rev. G. A.
STUDDERT
KENNEDY

Photo:
W. W. DOWTY, Worcester

Dr.
F. B. MEYER

Then came his services in the Operetta House, where he repeated the success and influence of Henry Drummond in his special ministry to students.   One of these students, now an honoured and well-known minister, writing shortly before Kelman's death, said: "It was perhaps inevitable that when I went to Edinburgh University about the year 1910, I should at once fall under the spell of Dr. John Kelman.   Everything about the great students' preacher fascinated me.   His transparent sincerity, his silver voice, the literary charm of his style, all combined to make him my idol. He gave to the ministry a new glory in my eyes.   That a man who was a very prince among men should be a minister did more than anything else to convince me that the preacher's is the grandest calling that any young man could choose to follow."   That tribute could be multiplied a hundredfold by Kelman's disciples, who have given full proof of their ministry throughout the world.

The next stage in his career was his colleagueship with Dr. Alexander Whyte in St. George's, Edinburgh.   It was a special joy to Dr. Whyte when, ultimately, he got as a colleague one whom he had been so eager to secure as an assistant.   Their twelve years' collaboration was of the happiest nature.   Kelman's preaching developed under the new conditions and his influence became wider than ever.

The late Earl of Rosebery, the outstanding Scotsman of his time, was one of Kelman's great admirers, and was often seen at the services in St. George's.   "Constantly," it has been said, "he sat at Kelman's feet, and he often sought his company at Dalmeny, and in his years of weary disability at The Durdans, Epsom."

It was typical of Kelman that he readily offered his services when the Great War broke out in 1914, and he not only ministered to the men at the Front, but he was sent on a special mission to America, where he thrilled vast audiences and did much to make that country realise the actual situation.

A serious breakdown in health, and the memory of his experiences in America, led to Kelman's acceptance of the call he had received from the famous Fifth Avenue Church, New York, to succeed Dr. J. H. Jowett, who was then returning to England. That was, perhaps, the greatest mistake he ever made, although he took the step in all good faith.   He arrived in New York a tired and an ill man, but he entered on his new duties with characteristic heroism.   His preaching made its own appeal, and he exercised as in Scotland a remarkable personal influence.   But the strain proved too great, and within five years he announced his resignation

and his intention of returning to the homeland.   For a year he held
the ministry of Frognal Presbyterian Church, London, but another
breakdown put an end to his active service. The last four years of
his life were spent in fighting pain and depression, with ups and
downs of strength, but without the hope of his being able to resume
the work of the ministry he had so greatly loved.

His death was profoundly mourned. It was a great loss to the
pulpit, for John Kelman was a preacher with a power peculiar to
himself.   His sermons, particularly in the earlier years of his
ministry, had a rich literary flavour. Many of his illustrations were
taken from the idols in the world of literature at that time—Robert
Louis Stevenson, Walter Pater, Matthew Arnold, Robert Browning. He seemed in those days to be, in a sense, a combination of
Henry Drummond and Robert Louis Stevenson. There was about
him something of Drummond's princely personality, and he had
Stevenson's delight in a "world that is full of a number of things." He
was an ardent Stevensonian, and one of the best of all his published
works was his volume on "The Faith of Robert Louis Stevenson."

But there was something far more than beauty and literary style
in Kelman's sermons.   In his preaching he had always one great
objective—to see Christ steadily and to see Him whole.   A well-
known writer once said of him, "It is the full-orbed complete
Christ he wants to present; the Son of Man Who touches life
at every point, who is not merely the *Christus Consolator*, or the
Lamb of God that taketh away sin, or the great Master who calls
His followers to self-denial and the bearing of the Cross, but also
the great Joy-bringer, the Intensifier of life, the supreme Incarnation of the will to live, or rather of God's will that man should
live, and live with abounding zest and joyous vigour. His presentation may be compared to a landscape in which all aspects and
moods of nature are found on one canvas.   The fury of the storm
and the peace of clear skies, the ominous shadow and the friendly
sunlight, the grandeur of rugged hills, and the prettiness of a flower
garden—all are in the picture.   The green pastures and still waters
verge on the valley of the shadow of death, and Calvary is set among
the kindly purple hills of home.   He does not want to paint only
quiet glades and laughing brooks.   'We have tethered Christ
among the lilies,' is a favourite phrase of his.   He wants to make
room in his presentation for the Agony and the Sacrifice, for man's
sin and God's passion. With a wealth of quiet insight and an
individual power of persuasion, he sets the complete Christ, the
Lord of all Life, before us."

It used to be said that Kelman "came into the pulpit with a rush like a racehorse eager for the contest." What many of us will always remember was his tall, spare, lithe figure—high strung, alive and vibrant in every fibre of his being. His personality had something at once noble and attractive that made its own appeal almost before he had uttered a word. And even after all he may have said, and said so earnestly and so impressively, with such ability and persuasive power, it was often the power of his personality that lingered with us above all else.

The organisation of his congregations never greatly interested him. He put his strength into his preaching and into personal intercourse with people. One of the secrets of his success with the students was his personal interest in them. His wife and he used to take groups of young students to their hospitable home on Sunday evening, and he often kept some of the fellows with him until the small hours of Monday morning, "talking on life in all its manifold aspects, and especially on life with Christ, its incalculable enricher."

And then Kelman was the incomparable pastor. He put himself utterly at the disposal of those who needed him when they were bowed down under sorrow or trials, visiting them indefatigably while their shadows lasted. Even those who had no claim on his services sought him out when they were overtaken by tragedy or loss as they instinctively felt that he was one on whose sympathy they could count, and he gave himself as freely to some wanderer from the ends of the earth as to a former Prime Minister. It was because of the way in which he walked with them in the hardest stretches of their life that so many learned to love John Kelman and so warmly treasure his memory still. The influence of these things they continue to feel after the eloquence of even his best sermons has been long forgotten.

April 1, 1939

XXXV

Dr. D. M. McINTYRE

IT was after a short, sharp illness that Dr. D. M. McIntyre passed to his rest. He had been laid aside only for a week. I had one of the last letters written by his own hand—perhaps it was the very last. And it was characteristic of him that it was saying something on behalf of a friend. Only a few days earlier, when he sent a letter thanking me for something he had appreciated, he remarked: "I hope you are battling bravely against the spring winds." Alas! that he should have fallen a victim to these winds.

In his small, neat, close handwriting Dr. McIntyre penned many kindly notes. I never knew him ask for publicity of any kind about himself, but I never knew him despise it in a superior sort of way as smaller souls are apt to do. Nor did I ever know him fail to acknowledge it. A review of one of his books, or a reference to his work, would invariably bring from him by first post a brief but kindly acknowledgment. He was the soul of courtesy, and he loved to say "Thank you."

It was a delight to have a conversation with him. He could talk interestingly with a quiet humour of his own. How free he was of the petty jealousies and littlenesses which disfigure some otherwise fine characters. With all his rigid views I never heard him utter a censorious word about anyone who had a wider oulook. It was this which made him so beloved by men of all schools of thought.

A son of the manse (his father was minister at Monikie), Dr. McIntyre was invited, while still a student, to be missionary in St. John's, Leith, under Dr. Kelman, father of Dr. John Kelman, afterwards of St. George's. Later he went to London, and for two years had charge of a Church Extension movement at College Park. On the conclusion of his Divinity course he was invited to be the first minister of the newly-sanctioned College Park congregation, and he spent five years in that charge.

In his congregation there he had the parents and grandparents of one who was afterwards to become a famous preacher—Dr. W. E. Orchard. I have heard him speak of the fine stock from which Dr. Orchard came. With Dr. Orchard himself, through the changes in his outlook and his ecclesiastical environment, even after his conversion to Roman Catholicism, Dr. McIntyre continued to the last to keep in touch, both personally and by correspondence. Dr. Orchard, on his part, has testified both publicly and privately to his lasting respect for Dr. McIntyre.

It was in 1891 that Dr. McIntyre came to Glasgow to be colleague and successor to the saintly Andrew A. Bonar, of Finnieston. It was an ideal colleagueship while it lasted, but it was destined to be of short duration, for Dr. Bonar died fifteen months later. Left as a young man with the burden of such a pastorate, Dr. McIntyre, in his own quiet way, soon proved equal to the occasion, and for over 20 years he not only maintained and increased the congregation but was also able to preserve most markedly the lofty spirit it had caught from Dr. Bonar.

When he became Principal of the Bible Training Institute in 1915 Dr. McIntyre continued (without emoluments) as senior minister of the congregation. With the Rev. William Simpson, who has since been acting minister, his relationship was such as to prove that colleagueships are not always a failure. Not so long ago Mr. Simpson described Dr. McIntyre as "the angel of the Church at Finnieston."

In the Bible Training Institute during the term of Dr. McIntyre's Principalship over 1000 students in residence have gone out to Christian service, and more than 500 of these are to be found in Foreign Mission fields all over the world. Thus did his influence permeate to the ends of the earth.

Dr. McIntyre's leanings theologically were definitely conservative. But he was never thirled to any particular school of thought; and this fact gave him an appeal which was almost universal, for he was welcomed in every circle, whether right wing or left wing. He became all things to all men without abating one jot of his own views or his personal sympathies. His faith was held with a certain large simplicity but absolute conviction. He dwelt in the positive.

Our first and last thought about him is that he was a Christian. With all the wide range of his knowledge and culture, it is not his gifts which seem to shine so much as his character. As minister of Finnieston and as Principal of the Bible Training Institute, he gave many men and women all the Christian teaching they are ever likely to know or to need, and in that way his influence will tell both at home and throughout the world for years to come. His numerous books, too, will keep his name alive. But perhaps the greatest influence of all was just that of the man himself. Wherever he went he carried an air and an atmosphere which could not but be felt.

I have never known anyone who had in greater degree than Dr. McIntyre what can only be called a perfect poise of personality. There was something so calm, so composed, about him as to be a rebuke to anything flurried or exciting. It was conspicuous alike in his casual conversation and in his public speech. He never lost his fine tranquillity.

As a preacher and speaker Dr. McIntyre attempted no flights beyond his own range. His voice had only a few notes, but that quiet, even voice could be very effective. He might be described as a master of the monotone, and he proved how even a monotone could become melodious and appealing. His own calm confidence in his message, his transparent sincerity, his unruffled victorious faith, his serenity of spirit, gradually wove a spell of persuasive power. In a very striking sense he always exemplified, in his preaching as in everything else about him, the truth of the promise that "in quietness and confidence shall be your strength."

At the celebration of his ministerial jubilee he said, "However imperfectly I have done it, I have always tried to present Christ in the glory of His person, and in the fulness and fruitfulness of His work." And he did it, not by his preaching only, but also by his personality. There could be no finer or more fitting epitaph for D. M. McIntyre than the lines:

> For us, 'twas not the truth you taught,
> To you so clear, to us so dim,
> But when you came to us, you brought
> A sense of Him.

November 12, 1938

XXXVI

Professor W. P. PATERSON

IN the death of Professor W. P. Paterson we have lost one of whom it can be said without any exaggeration that we shall not look upon his like again. He stood out unique and distinctive in an age characterised by standardised types of personality and gifts.

There was a peculiar fascination about Professor Paterson. Even his eccentricities were attractive, for they were the eccentricities of genius, and his mannerisms were a constant delight to witness. *Punch* once said that Dr. John Clifford wore two ties, one in front and one behind, and that when he got wound up in some great speech the ties made a complete tour of his person and ultimately recovered their original positions. The story might have been equally true of Professor Paterson if he had worn ties and not clerical collars. He was not only regardless but blissfully unconscious of his personal appearance.

His absent-mindedness became proverbial and gave rise to innumerable stories which have been told with delight in circles all over the country. Many of them may be mythical, but some are undoubtedly founded on fact, and in any case they have become cherished traditions with which we would be fain to part. He was quite aware of how they went the round, and I remember him telling me long ago that the story of a minister who set out on a journey by train and wired his wife from a junction asking where he was going was not true in his case, although he always enjoyed hearing it told.

As a theologian his pre-eminence was everywhere acknowledged. From his article on "Jesus Christ" in Hastings' one-volume *Bible Dictionary* to his great Gifford Lectures on "The Nature of Religion," he built up a reputation which will last for generations.

The late Lord Sands once said of Professor Paterson that, like Bacon, he took all knowledge for his subject. Genius has been described by Canon Scott Holland as being "the persistence in grown men of the spirit of the child—of the child's naïve simplicity, inexhaustible freshness and wistful eagerness to learn." How aptly the description applied to Professor Paterson! A wistful eagerness to learn was characteristic of him to the last. It used to be said that Lord Rosebery was "the orator of the Empire" because of the facility and felicity with which he could speak on any subject, familiar or otherwise. Professor Paterson's versatility was such that the same could have been said of him. There was no subject on which he could not discourse with brilliance and originality.

It was surprising to find that this profound thinker was at the same time one of the most playful and whimsical of speakers. On the public platform or on the floor of the General Assembly there was none to compare with him. His presence in the Assembly was welcomed as that of no other man of his time. As he came tripping into the Hall with his light, quick step he would be pointed out by members in the body of the House and by the general public in the galleries. And when he intervened in a debate there was a visible quickening of interest, whatever the subject. It was like what happens in the House of Commons when a "star" speaker gets on his feet and the benches quickly fill up. The news that "W. P." was speaking went round the lobbies and corridors of the Assembly Hall and everyone was eager to hear him.

In a description of him penned on one such occasion it was said: "Sometimes both hands were in his trouser pockets, then one hand would be rumpling his thick crop of white hair or sawing the air in emphatic argument as he passed from incidental particulars to wide generalisations, from gay to grave, dropping by the way suggestive *obiter dicta* or curious *minutiæ* of information." An old professional colleague said many years ago: "Professor Paterson touches no subject without shedding light upon it from the fire of his own individuality. However old the question might be, he never repeats the conventional commonplaces; he always says the unexpected; and usually the unexpected approves itself as the inevitable."

I recall an occasion when he had been summoned to preach before King George V and Queen Mary in Crathie Parish Church. Such an experience is trying, and to some extent unsettling, to most ministers, but Professor Paterson seemed supremely unconcerned. There was the usual crowded congregation; the King was in the centre of the Royal pew with the Queen and the Prince of Wales on his right and Princess Mary on his left, while in the pews immediately behind was the party from the Castle, which included some distinguished figures, both home and foreign.

The service was conducted by Dr. S. J. Ramsay Sibbald, then

PROFESSOR W. P. PATERSON

To face page 132

minister of the parish, who wore the robes of a Chaplain to the King in Scotland, and several medals and decorations. Professor Paterson was simply attired in his black Geneva gown and bands. He had been sitting, evidently lost in thought, until the time came for him to ascend the pulpit. He announced his text, and at once plunged into his sermon, and one soon felt that for him it was not a case of delivering a sermon before Royalty, but of preaching a sermon to a congregation. He preached as naturally, as fervently, and as definitely as his wont, quite unimpressed by the stately surroundings. It was a sermon which arrested and held the attention of hearers of all social grades. It had perhaps one limitation—it lasted only twenty-two minutes, barely half the Professor's average—and one felt that the curtailment must have been somewhat hampering to the preacher himself.

As a preacher, Professor Paterson was like no other. He had copied no man's method, and it would have been fatal—even if it had been possible—for anyone to attempt to copy his. Of his power in the pulpit there could be no question. He combined intellectual strength and brilliance with fervency of spirit and utterance. The slight burr in his speech was no drawback; it seemed rather to increase the effect. Using nothing in the way of manuscript or notes, his words flowed on in finely-marshalled sentences and terse, epigrammatic sayings. During the delivery of the sermon his eyes were often closed as he stood wrestling with his theme and working it out with masterly skill, to arrest, convince, and persuade his hearers. It was a sight to be remembered—the utter abandon of the preacher and the rapt attention of a congregation as it sat under his grip.

With advancing years Professor Paterson came to have more and more a serenity of expression which seemed to indicate that he was living in a realm far above all that was petty and passing. He was always quick in his movements, and death came to him in like manner. On the last day of his life he had been up and about, and when he retired to rest it was to awaken no more on this side. Now his eager, questing spirit will be reaching out for further experiences.

What lands shall greet your gaze?
What winds shall lift your hair?
What mightier stars for you shall blaze
In what diviner air?

January 14, 1939

XXXVII

Dr. F. B. MEYER

IN course of his "persistent peregrinations" at home and abroad, Dr. F. B. Meyer was a fairly frequent visitor to Glasgow. Even to extreme old age he was one of the greatest of "globe-trotters." The wanderlust was in his blood.

Once when visiting Sir William Robertson Nicoll, he told his host how he envied him his immense library, how greatly he wished he might have leisure to browse among the books. Nicoll rather upset his exclamations of delight by saying: "Now you know, Meyer, you would not be here an hour before you would be asking for a Bradshaw's Railway Guide." It was taken in good part, and they joined in a hearty laugh. A writer, knowing nothing of this incident, once spoke of Meyer as "St. Francis with a Bradshaw." Some of us can still recall an article entitled "The Devil Disguised as a Railway Train," with special reference to the danger of Dr. Meyer wearing himself out in meeting countless demands for his services in all parts of the country. These criticisms never upset him; he kept on his way unconcernedly, and he could stand the strain of railway journeying better than most men.

Yet it cannot be questioned that his mode of life had an effect on his preaching. Someone once speculated on the heights which he might have scaled had he specialised in preaching after the severe and exclusive manner of J. H. Jowett. That, however, was not his way. He was many other things besides a preacher. A man of action to the finger-tips he could never have been content merely to proclaim a message from his pulpit. He had to be up and doing. At the same time Meyer at his greatest was a preacher of peculiar and compelling power. There was something about the man himself which was impressive in no ordinary degree.

His face has been described as a spiritual landscape; "life, the sculptor, having made it into a calm and serene poetry of contour." He came of Quaker ancestry, and it has been said that his calm, benignant expression might have justified that saying of Charles Lamb, "I have seen faces in their assemblies upon which the dove sat visibly brooding." One who knew him well remarked, "He would have worn an archbishop's cope and mitre with natural grace, or even the Papal tiara.   What a portrait of him might have been handed down from the age of Titian!"   Particularly in his later years there was a saintliness about him which could not but be felt.

Of the occasions on which I heard Dr. Meyer, two stand out specially in my memory.   The circumstances and surroundings were as different as could possibly have been imagined.   One was in London when he was minister of Regent's Park Chapel. His work there was more circumscribed than in Christ Church. It was a smaller building and with a district congregation rather than a miscellaneous crowd.   Into that setting, however, he seemed to fit as perfectly as if it had been made for him.

Quietly, persuasively, serenely, and in silver tones he proclaimed his message.   The phrasing was simple, with the simplicity of the art which conceals art, the imagery peaceful and pastoral "like an English valley washed with sunlight."   He held aloft a winsome Saviour, the Christ whose healing dress is ever by our beds of pain, who brings comfort and consolation to stricken souls. Everything was intimate, tender, and appealing.   It was truly said of him that his was the grand manner that could be intimate without a suspicion of impertinence, and whose familiarity bred no contempt, while there was consummate ease and subtle mastery of effect in his manipulation of speech and thought.

The other occasion I specially recall was when he had come to give the closing address at the World's Sunday School Convention in Glasgow in 1924.   St. Andrew's Hall was crowded to its utmost capacity with a magnificent audience, and the atmosphere was tense as matters moved to a climax.

Dr. Meyer's address was already in type, but, sensing the situation, he scrapped what he had prepared and addressed himself direct to his hearers, gathering up all the threads of the Convention with a deftness which had a touch of real inspiration.   It was a personal talk more moving than the most thrilling oratory.

Dr. Meyer was then rather feeble in body, and a high stool had been provided, on which he could sit behind a desk when addressing the meeting.   But he forgot all about the special provision which had been made for his comfort; his spirit triumphed over his physical weakness.   As he spoke, his very countenance seemed transfigured; with radiant face and in a quiet, gracious way he led the vast audience towards a great final act of dedication.   At the close he restrained with uplifted hand a burst of applause, and then there rolled forth the triumphant notes of the Hallelujah

Chorus, which gave vent to the pent-up emotion of his hearers. It was an unforgettable scene.

In certain circles the name of F. B. Meyer stood for what was regarded as light-weight Evangelism. But that only revealed a failure to realise the real power of the man. His preaching, tested by its results, was far from ordinary. His work profoundly affected countless lives. And he will always be remembered for his real saintliness—not that he was a plaster saint, for he was very human. He had a keen sense of humour and a good story gave him real enjoyment.

Dr. Parker expressed the minds of many when he said: "He brings a benediction with him, a better air than earth's poor murky climate, and he never leaves me without the impression that I have been face to face with a man of God." And it was because of this that he was able to throw such a vision on the drab canvas of our common life, and became one of the preachers who could lead the souls of men out of the shadow into the sunlight of eternal love.

November 4, 1939

XXXVIII

Rev. G. A. STUDDERT KENNEDY

PROBABLY no Chaplain to the Forces identified himself more closely with the men on service or gained a greater influence over them than did the Rev. G. A. Studdert Kennedy. But he had proved his power first of all in the ministry at home.

At Rugby, then as curate to his father in Leeds, and finally at Worcester, Studdert Kennedy revealed his unique gifts. It was at Worcester that he acquired such a personal hold over the soldiers as made it imperative he should be sent to the Front. He had been invited by the Dean to preach at a parade service in the Cathedral, with the result that thereafter, Sunday after Sunday, he spoke to 2000 men of the Forces, not only holding them spellbound at the time, but giving them something to think about which became the main topic of conversation for the following week.

With all his extraordinary preaching gifts, Studdert Kennedy had also the pastoral instinct to a degree not usually found among popular preachers. He loved all sorts and conditions of men and women, and was naturally interested in them. There was nowhere he would hesitate to go in order to get in touch with them.

"I can see again," said one of his friends, "that small, slim figure strolling into the unattractive public house where his beloved lodging-house tramps were to be found, and standing up at the bar in his cassock to sing 'Nazareth,' while half his audience 'felt within a power unfelt before.' They loved him—loved him for his great laugh, the smile that transformed his face, the inimitable Irish brogue, but most of all because of his love of them. He was entirely at home in the dirtiest of kitchens, and would sit for hours talking or watching by a sick-bed forgetting in all probability some important engagement elsewhere."

When he was preaching or speaking he became so absorbed as to be quite unconscious of himself and his actions. I remember hearing him at a great meeting in the Usher Hall, Edinburgh. When he began his address, he was standing at the side of the platform table; in a short time he was half-sitting on the edge of the table with one leg dangling; and thus he remained, evidently quite oblivious of the strange spectacle he presented. But how he thrilled his hearers with his burning, consuming earnestness!

He was utterly and uncompromisingly realistic. And he set himself deliberately to capture attention by a startling introductory remark and he would use a very daring phrase in order to emphasise a point or to make a truth memorable to his hearers.

It would be easy to criticize the language he often used—language like that of his very vivid and often daring "Rough Rhymes of a Padre." To some extent it was in keeping with his passionate prayer:

> O by Thy Cross and Passion, Lord!
> By broken hearts that pant
> For comfort and for love of Thee,
> Deliver us from cant.

One of his friends has said: "There is no doubt that in the eyes of many this constant use of forcible and startling expressions amounted to weakness. Others preferred to look upon it as an anomaly which, in his case, was used entirely for good. While in some cases it is clear that his hearers did not distinguish his own words from those quotations of the language of the men which he so freely employed, there were many who tried to persuade him that his message would have gone home just as forcibly without such expletives. But perhaps we were wrong: he maintained that those in his audiences who took offence were seeking to dodge the issue."

On one occasion he all unconsciously so moved the soldiers that they were cheering Christ. At a Good Friday sermon he had held the crowd in rapt attention for an hour as he preached on the message of the Cross. At the close "there was the awe, the hush, the silence, and then the roar, and it meant real homage to Christ from men who were, hundreds of them, going to the death." Studdert Kennedy himself was taken aback. "It sounded strange," he wrote home, "to hear men cheer Christ, strange to us and not perhaps what we would do, but you would have loved it, and so, I am sure, did He."

Studdert Kennedy had the gift of eloquence, and even of oratory that was fiery and provocative and compelling. But not the least element in his power was his utter sincerity and a certain fragrance of unconscious goodness.

He was certainly one of the discoveries of the great war of 1914-1918. It was then that he earned the name "Woodbine Willie," given to him by the soldiers at the Front, to whom he handed out Testaments with one hand and cigarettes with the other. He himself wrote of it:

> They gave me this name like their nature,
> Compacted of laughter and tears,
> A sweet that was born of the bitter,
> A joke that was torn from the years!

He was unique in personality and gifts, and distinctly unconventional. He copied no one, and did not expect any one to copy him. No matter how people disliked his nickname, or disapproved of his actions, he believed in the course he had taken, and nothing could deflect him from that course. His fearlessness, his sincerity, and his detestation of hypocrisy and cant were among his shining characteristics which even those who differed from him were compelled to admit.

One of the least likely to be impressed by a man of Studdert Kennedy's type would be the Archbishop of Canterbury (Dr. Temple), and he confessed that until he met him he had been as much repelled as attracted by his utterances. But from their first meeting he fell under the spell of "Woodbine Willie" because of his intense reality and his intimate and complete dedication.

"If," said the Archbishop, "to be a priest is to carry others on the heart and offer them with self in the sacrifice of human nature to God the Father of our Lord Jesus Christ, then Geoffrey Studdert Kennedy was the finest priest I have known."

Having never learned to husband the taper, his life flickered out when he was only 46. But Studdert Kennedy had run a great race, and there was a breath of life's morning about him to the very last.

After making every allowance for the individualism, originality, and perhaps even the eccentricity of Studdert Kennedy, it may truly be said that he was a great preacher, for he got his message home to the hearts of hearers whom he had specially in view, and who would have remained untouched, unaffected, and unreached, had they not heard this forceful, flaming evangelist with a style all his own.

January 17, 1942

XXXIX

Rev. WILLIAM STODDART

REV. WILLIAM STODDART was a native of Kelso, where his father was a revered home missionary, and he studied at Edinburgh University and New College. His contemporaries in New College still tell of how he swept the boards in the final year. This dreamy student was interested in many other things than Divinity and, in particular, was passionately fond of literature and seemingly indifferent to his place in the classes. But by a few days of hard study immediately before the examination, he so completely mastered the subjects as to win the Cunningham Fellowship, awarded to the most distinguished student leaving the Divinity Hall.

After a brief assistantship to Dr. Hugh Macmillan in what was then the West Church, Greenock, Mr. Stoddart was ordained at Innellan in 1898, but within three years of his settlement he accepted a call to Trinity Church, Aberdeen. There he entered on what was unquestionably the greatest period of his life. From the outset he caught the ear of the city. His preaching made, indeed, quite a sensation. Sunday after Sunday extra seats had to be provided in the church to accommodate the crowds, even the pulpit steps being occupied, while his sermons became topics of general discussion in the city.

When he came to Partick in 1911 he was faced with entirely different circumstances. In Aberdeen he could command the whole city; in Partick he had only a district constituency. During the 25 years of his ministry there he witnessed the steady migration of people to the outer fringes of the city with all its discouragements to those in the centre. He had also his own personal sorrows, but he kept bravely on his way and the old radiant spirit still shone forth, especially in the company of congenial friends. Mr. Stoddart had a very attractive personality once he was known, with an irresistible sense of humour, and in all his congregations he made friendships which have endured.

Like his sister, Miss Jane T. Stoddart, of *The British Weekly*, the most accomplished lady journalist of her day, Mr. Stoddart was a master of literary style. His insatiable love of literature in all its forms, from the classical to the popular, was always character-istic of the man. He was far more observant of life than many who did not fully know him ever realized, and everything he picked up, whether in life or literature, was grist to his mill as a preacher.

In his preaching he had a wide range of style. From a pungent polemic on some moral issue, he could pass with seeming ease to an earnest Evangelical discourse, or to a sermon couched in language fit to rank as prose poetry. He had often a wistful note, for the tragedy and pathos of life touched him to the quick, and with a tender touch and a swell in his voice he could deeply move his hearers.

In his prime, he was as fine a sermon-maker as I have ever heard. Every discourse was a work of art as well as a glowing deliverance. He believed in three "heads" and they were always apt and often alliterative. His familiar phrasing was "firstly; secondly and more briefly; thirdly and in a word." He never elaborated his points, but when he finished one felt there was no more to be said.

It is a great tribute to any preacher that many years afterwards people still speak of his sermons and even quote some of his divisions. That is the case with hearers of Mr. Stoddart. "Do you remember?" one will ask the other, and then they go on to exchange reminiscences of never-to-be-forgotten days in packed pews. Among his great sermons were those on "A sea of glass mingled with fire," "Days of heaven upon earth," "The glorious Lord will be unto us a place of broad rivers and streams."

A sermon of a different type was on "The Tongue," and it has never been forgotten, because of the impression made by the lines with which it closed and the tone in which they were uttered:

> Then in a nobler, sweeter song,
> I'll sing Thy power to save,
> When this poor lisping stammering tongue
> Lies silent in the grave.

At the time, delivered as they were with throbbing emotion as the climax to a great sermon, they had a dramatic effect; to-day they have a new and deeper significance.

December 28, 1935

XL

Dr. MARCUS DODS

NO man who afterwards rose to fame was ever so near being a "stickit minister" as Marcus Dods. After he had completed with high distinction his course of training he wandered in the wilderness for six years as a probationer preaching in vacancy after vacancy without success. He wrote to his friend, Mr. Taylor Innes, with a touch of sardonic humour, that he was meditating a discourse on the sick man at the Pool of Bethesda, adding: "He, however, had thirty-eight disappointments; I only twenty-one as yet."

But there were others still to follow. As a matter of fact, he had twenty-three distinct chances of more or less attractive charges and twenty-three times he lost. Dods had indeed come to be the chronic probationer of whom it has been said that "his worn bag with its two 'dried tongues' is the jest even of railway porters, his successive failures are known to every beadle in the land, and as the churchless years go by he becomes the shunned of sessions, the despised of Presbyteries, and the despair of ecclesiastics."

It said much for the audacity and faith and vision of a Glasgow congregation that it "took to its arms the disheartened residuum of three and twenty vacancies." But its reward was as great as its discernment. For a quarter of a century Marcus Dods made Renfield Church (in Bath Street at the corner of Elmbank Street) a great centre of light and leading in the religious life of the community. And he left it only when he was appointed a Professor in New College, Edinburgh, where later he also became Principal.

Yet it was not altogether surprising that Dods had such a long period of waiting, for it must be admitted that his style as a preacher was not attractive. Anyone more motionless in the pulpit it would have been difficult to imagine. Even when preaching his great sermons he used to stand apparently as immovable as a rock. The story is told of how a friend once urged him to introduce a gesture now and then. In his next sermon he managed to raise his hand at a certain point, but there it remained; he was unable to get it down again until the sermon was at an end!

It was also easy for his hearers at first to mistake the massiveness of his thought for heaviness. He was singularly devoid of artifice of any kind; even literary embellishment, though within his reach as within the reach of few, he disdained to use.

No better pen-picture of Marcus Dods has ever been given than by Professor Henry Drummond when he wrote: "He stands squarely in the pulpit, without either visible motion or emotion, reads his sermon from start to finish, without a pause, begins without awakening any sense of expectation, gives no hint throughout of either discovery or originality, however much the discourse may seem to teem with both, passes at a pace which never changes, in a voice without passion, or pathos, or cadence, or climax, through each of the half-dozen massive paragraphs of which every sermon is composed, and finishes bluntly when the last thing has been said, as if he were now well out of it for the week.

"But, on thinking over it when you go home, you perceive that the after-result is almost in proportion to the unconsciousness of the effect at the time. You know exactly why the sermon stopped just then; there was nothing more to be said; the proof was final. You discover easily why the appeal did not move you more. You have been accustomed to the sounds of passion vibrating in the chords of another soul. Now your own soul seethes and trembles. These effects are not the work of a man: they are the operating of the Spirit of Truth.

"You know at last why the man was so hidden, why he had no cunning phrases, why beautiful words do not linger in your memory, why a preacher so impersonal, and to whom you were so impersonal, a preacher so wholly uninterested in you, so innocent himself of taking you by the throat, has yet taken his subject by the throat and planted it down before your inmost being, so that you cannot get rid of it. You know that you have heard no brilliant or awakening oratory; but you feel that you have been searched and overawed, that unseen realities have looked you in the eyes and asked you questions and made you a more humble and a more obedient man."

There never was a more diligent worker than Marcus Dods. Charles Wesley complained in his diary that he fell from his horse and was sore injured, "which prevented me writing hymns *till next day*." The friends of Dods would have been alarmed to think of the consequences if he had been denied his favourite blue-grey quarto and broad-nibbed pen for two successive mornings. By his own admission, he loved to write; he said the exercise of the pen was a pleasure to him. Even before he got a church he had published two books, and he continued to produce volume after

volume until his working days were done.   His notable contributions to theological literature made other preachers his debtors,
but it is with his own preaching we are here concerned.

As long as he was in the ministry he allowed nothing to interfere
with the duty he owed to his congregation.   He toiled on methodi-
cally, preparing as faithfully for his week-night prayer meeting as
for the Sunday services.   What may seem surprising is that a special
feature of his Glasgow ministry in its later years was his monthly
talk to children.

The heresy hunts in which Marcus Dods figured are now happily
almost completely forgotten.   He had his critics, but the fact that
an Evangelical stalwart like Dr. Alexander Whyte, of St. George's,
Edinburgh, was all along his most intimate friend counted for a
great deal.   His sincerity was always transparent.   Sir William
Robertson Nicoll declared that he was the most Christlike man he
had ever known.

No one could desire a finer epitaph than that pronounced on
Marcus Dods when it was said: "What his people remember, what
his students bless him for, was the impression he left with them of
the tremendous reality of the spiritual life, the grandeur and inexhaustible glory of Christianity, the necessity and urgency of consecrated service, the stimulus to holy living to be found, and to be
found alone, in personal contact with Christ crucified and risen."

February 23, 1940

DR. DINSDALE T. YOUNG

To face page 144

XLI

Dr. DINSDALE T. YOUNG

DR. DINSDALE T. YOUNG was a man of remarkable gifts and of attractive personality. I heard him at different times in Glasgow, and I heard him at the Methodist Central Hall, Westminster, where he reigned for long like a king upon his throne.

I also met him on several occasions behind the scenes and the more I saw of him in private the better I liked him. He put on no airs: he was natural, unassuming and kindly to a degree; and his conversation so rich in reminiscence and anecdote was always a delight. He could be playful and humorous to a degree.

There was nothing ethereal about Dinsdale Young. He had a sweet tooth, especially for chocolates. He loved a good cigar, and could smoke almost any kind of pipe—being like Spurgeon in saying he enjoyed these to "the glory of God." But he declined to be seen smoking on the street.

What a picture he made, always moving with a certain native grandeur and invariably wearing his frock coat and silk hat. No one could have imagined Dinsdale Young attired in a jacket suit and soft hat. He grew old picturesquely, his white locks streaming out behind as if he were the Abbé Liszt, while two triangles of white hair flanked the high pink dome of his forehead.

He was a minister of the old school in his theology and preaching, and he gloried in the title. And when some people hinted at his narrowness, he was ready to reply that he could claim to have studied both sides more thoroughly than those who were supposed to be modern. And minister of the old school as he was he did not fail to attract young people. His popularity was phenomenal. Wherever he went, and he was constantly travelling all over the country, crowds flocked to hear him. When he was a minister in Edinburgh it was in the days when Alexander Whyte and Henry Drummond were the great magnets, but Dinsdale Young's congregations were unaffected. In the Central Hall, Westminster, he preached for 25 years, not only to the largest congregations in London, but to the largest in Britain. It is told of Dr. J. H. Jowett that, when minister of Westminster Chapel, he once asked an office-bearer why so many people always arrived

some twenty minutes after the service opened and were distributed
throughout such vacant seats as were left.   It was rather a shock to
him to be told that they were the overflow from Dinsdale Young's
Central Hall crowd.

A glorious voice, wonderfully used, was one of Dinsdale Young's
great gifts.   It was an organ voice, and it was said that, by his remarkable control of it, he could have electrified a congregation
just by his sounding forth of the word "Mesopotamia." There was
something rich, full, and resonant in its tones.   He had all the arts
of a speaker and such a supreme mastery of them as entirely concealed the art.

As to his method of preparation, his biographer, Mr. Harold
Murray, has said: "Having got his text, he went straight to the best
commentaries he could find on his well-lined library shelves.   In
many a sermon he would dwell on a word that had arrested him,
and then say, 'I went at once to ———.'   He always had a special
and rather uncommon delight in reading commentaries.   All
those who heard Dr. Young preach will remember how often
(dare one say too often?) he mentioned his delight in John Calvin,
Matthew Henry, Adam Clarke, above all, Thomas Goodwin, with
regard to whom he kept a special notebook crammed with choice
extracts.   His guides included Dr. Pusey, Bishop Lightfoot,
Bishop Westcott, Bishop Moule, even George Adam Smith, whose
Higher Critical views he vigorously rejected.   And of course he
frequently consulted the writings of Spurgeon, Newman, Dean
Vaughan, and Alexander McLaren."

I once heard him say that biography yielded him many of his
best illustrations, and that Dr. Andrew Bonar's Diary was one of
the books he read every year.   But his reading was not wholly
confined to the Puritans.   He ranged over the whole field of
literature.   He liked the novels of Mrs. Oliphant, Miss Braddon,
Wilkie Collins, Anthony Trollope, and George Meredith.   He once
told Rev. C. Ensor Walters that he enjoyed Edgar Wallace!

Dr. Young was said to have preached on over 700 texts at
Wesley's Chapel, and some thousands of texts at the Central Hall,
and yet he rarely re-treated the same one.   Of course he used
familiar sermons when travelling over the country, and he used to
cover thousands of miles a year.   He was "an inveterate homile-
tician."   He clung to the principle of firstly, secondly, and thirdly,
saying that Dr. McLaren's "three-pronged fork was a useful instrument."

Mr. Bardsley Brash has said that Dinsdale Young is described in that lovely book of George Herbert, "A Priest of the Temple, or the Country Parson," where it is said: "The Country Parson preacheth constantly, the pulpit is his joy, and his throne.   When he preacheth he procures attention by all possible art."

"Preaching as an ordinance," said Dr. Young, "is part of 'God's good pleasure.' There has been no revocation of this supreme ordinance. It is *the* Sacrament. Of all the acts of worship it is the most helpful. The churches grieve God's Spirit when they ignore or depreciate preaching." But he made every part of the service effective. He would say, "Let us now worship as we sing," and then he would read out the first verse in such a way as to make sure a familiar hymn shed some new glory. And after an anthem such as "How lovely are the messengers," his extempore prayer would be built upon it, and he would ring the changes on "the gospel of peace" in the most moving and memorable way.

Fundamentalist as he was, Dinsdale Young did not bother crossing swords with Modernists, and many who disagreed with his views were always to be found enjoying his preaching. He did not argue, he proclaimed. He was not an apologist, but a herald. He knew no hesitancies or wistful doubts but preached with all his soul a gospel of grace abounding to the chief of sinners. What a thrill it was to hear him quote, as his own experience, William Cowper's lines:

> E'er since by faith I saw the stream
> Thy flowing wounds supply,
> Redeeming love has been my theme,
> And shall be till I die.

The last time I heard him in public he concluded thus: "Brethren, hope perfectly. Let us ring out our Rabbi Ben Ezra watchword, 'The best is yet to be'."

The great preacher's faith did not fail him at the last. During moments of consciousness, as he lay awaiting the final call, he continually repeated lines of the hymn, "Just as I am," and his last distinguishable words were, "I triumph."

January 29, 1938

XLII

Professor H. R. MACKINTOSH

FEW men have been more missed or more sincerely mourned than Professor Hugh R. Mackintosh. Since his death on June 8, 1936, many have expressed the hope that there might be some fitting memorial of the man and his work. That hope is realised by the publication of a volume of his sermons, with a memoir by Emeritus-Professor A. B. Macaulay (T. and T. Clark, Edinburgh, 7s.).

Professor Macaulay had unique qualifications for this labour of love. "Hugh Ross Mackintosh," he says, "was my intimate and dear friend for nearly fifty years. It is not easy for me to give an entirely objective appreciation of his personality and a completely impartial appreciation of his work. We knew each other well; we had few secrets which we did not share with one another; our friendship was a rare and close fellowship of mind and heart."

I think every reader will agree that this Memoir could not have been better done. It is quite true that Professor Macaulay writes as a friend, but it needed a friend who knew and understood Professor Mackintosh as he really was to give us this revealing delineation of the man. There is no extravagance of statement; it is a studied and just appraisement written with deep feeling and many a tender touch.

The facts of Professor Mackintosh's career are well known—his birth in Paisley; his extraordinarily brilliant record as a student; his ministries in Tayport and Aberdeen; his Professorship in New College, Edinburgh, for 32 years; his Moderatorship of the Church of Scotland in 1932; his world-wide fame as a theologian by reason of his many published works. He seemed the natural person to succeed Principal Martin in the Principalship of New College and, says Professor Macaulay, "he would probably have done so had New College remained a separate institution. In the scheme of amalgamation the offices of Principal of New College and Dean of the Faculty of Divinity were, rightly or wrongly, combined. To Hugh it was a genuine relief that he was not appointed to this dual post with its multifarious duties."

Many who knew Mackintosh only as a theologian and a Church-

Rev.
WILLIAM STODDART

Photo:
LAFAYETTE, Ltd., Glasgow

Dr.
MARCUS DODS

Photo:
R. S. FORREST, Edinburgh

To face page 148

Professor
H. R. MACKINTOSH

Photo:
A. SWAN WATSON, Edinburgh

Pastor
D. J. FINDLAY

Photo:
LAFAYETTE, Ltd., Glasgow

man will be glad to get glimpses of him behind the scenes. We are told that "unduly absent-minded he was not, unlike some of his professorial contemporaries. Occasionally, however, he did absent-minded things. For instance, he turned up to a levee at Buckingham Palace without a ticket, and had to trust to his tricorn and the lace on his coat as credentials of his title to obtain entrance. And—palaces seemed to have scared him—once when he was on a visit to the Archbishop of Canterbury *en route* for Hungary he left his reserve of clerical collars behind him at Lambeth Palace."

It is said, however, that "he conformed fully to the traditional professorial type in his earnest simplicity. It was a charming feature of the man, as charming as his native Highland courtesy, and it explained the affection which he drew from everyone with whom he came in contact. (He never passed a hospital nurse or a Church sister without raising his hat.) Only," adds his biographer, "he was none the worse of having a sophisticated friend at his side when a beggar accosted him, or a smart salesman got into 'gear' over the virtues of a motor car which Hugh seemed to fancy."

An incessant worker, who "hadn't an idle bone in his body," he was yet able to relax. "He enjoyed attending the concerts for which Edinburgh is famous, and seldom missed a good ' picture.' Latterly he became fond of motoring, and without being, or professing to be, anything of a mechanic, he could drive a car with complete safety to himself and his passengers. His favourite recreations were football and golf. The former he played occasionally when he was a student, but up to the last he was an eager follower of the game in both its forms, Association and Rugby."

Professor Mackintosh had an extraordinarily wide knowledge of detective fiction, rivalling and even excelling the remarkable record in this respect of Professor James Moffatt.

He is said to have been without talent as a wit, while enjoying the witticisms of others, but he had a keen sense of humour and an uninhibited cheerful laugh. As a raconteur he had few equals. His repertoire was extensive. Here are two examples quoted by Professor Macaulay :

' He was fond of telling how, soon after his marriage, one of the members of his Fife congregation, happening to meet him, asked him how he was enjoying married life. 'Very well,' answered Hugh. 'Ay,' said the Fifer, 'merridge is man's inclination and God's will, an' it's no' often thae twa things chime thegither.'

"Another story which he told, with a rare aptitude for imitating the Northern accent, was about an aged Highland minister of the 'old school' whom he was in the habit of visiting.   On one occasion his host confided to Hugh that there were three places into which, he was thankful to say, he had never been tempted to go: 'a theatre, a U.P. kirk, and a bath!'"

"A genuine scholar, a man of immense and accurate learning," Mackintosh is also described as "one supremely sensitive to the Divine, a man 'apart' who walked with God, transparently devout and dedicated."   Here is a description by an old student of the effect produced by one of his class-room lectures on the Atonement—"Step by step he had led us into the great deeps where we knew the abasement of our sin, and thought of the love of God that could reach even deeper than our sin.   After it was all over, some members of the class started to stamp their feet in loud applause.   Professor Mackintosh looked up dismayed.   He flung out an appealing hand, and the stamping died away.   'Ah no, gentlemen,' he said, 'I feel rather that I should engage in an act of penitence for daring to handle such things as these.'"   Another old student tells how on a similar occasion the Professor raised his head quietly and said, "Ah, gentlemen, let us not applaud, let us rather worship."

Of Mackintosh's preaching, Professor Macaulay says: "He could preach effectively 'without paper,' but he usually read his discourses from a manuscript.   His delivery was in conformity with what I may call the traditional New College manner; he never shouted and he never used a gesture.   His voice was a beautiful baritone, and he could make himself heard without effort.   For effects, from an extraneous point of view, he trusted to lucidity, distinction in phraseology, and to a quiet and reverent utterance. There was nothing about his speech to put hearers off; there was everything short of oratory to attract them.   In their substance his sermons owed a good deal directly to the influence of Principal Martin and Dr. Charles Watson; in their substance and form a good deal indirectly to the influence of that prince of preachers, Dr. Alexander McLaren, of Manchester."

This exactly expresses what I remember of Professor Mackintosh's preaching from the many occasions on which I heard him. Never was there anything less sensational; it was not even popular in the generally accepted sense of that term.   Yet it was preaching that gripped and held the attention of old and young, of the learned and the unlearned, although it was devoid of every effort of an external kind.   Could there be greater proof of its real power?

XLIII

Pastor D. J. FINDLAY

WHEN the news of Pastor Findlay's death became known it was recognised on every hand, and by men and women of all shades of opinion, that a great and notable figure had passed away. It was felt that it meant more than the loss of a leader in the evangelical life of the community; it was like the removal of a local landmark familiar to more than one generation of the citizens.

Pastor Findlay was a Glasgow man in every fibre of his being. He had spent all his long life in the city; had figured in some stirring years in its history more than half a century ago; and was one of the few remaining links with that period, which left such an abiding influence in the community. Moreover, his own personality had made such an impression with the passing years that there had gathered around it traditions known everywhere. He had become, as it were, an established institution, familiar by name and reputation to all ranks and classes. And so, as men said one to another, "Pastor Findlay is dead," they forgot all the points on which, in belief and otherwise, they may have differed from him, and were ready to unite with one voice in the tribute that "a prince and a great man is fallen this day in Israel."

The story of Mr. Findlay's career is so well known as to require no recapitulation here. Let me, therefore, refer rather to some of the characteristics of this remarkable man which made him what he was.

I can well remember the occasion, many years ago, when I first met Mr. Findlay face to face. It was in his room at the Tabernacle, which was also his office, where he was accustomed to spend his time at that big desk dealing personally with his heavy correspondence from all parts of the world. He disdained the assistance of typists and typewriters and up to the last wrote all his hundreds, if not thousands, of letters in that strong, bold handwriting so familiar to many.

My first impression of him at close quarters dispelled some illusions. I found him more genial than I expected from his public appearances. From then onwards we were frequently in close contact and I got to know him in private as well as in public.

There were many points on which we could never have seen eye to eye, but we knew and respected each other's point of view, and our friendship was not in any way affected. Whatever my feeling as to some of his opinions and as to his general outlook, I always had a profound respect for his sterling sincerity and an admiration for the strength of his convictions. It was impossible not to feel how much richer we would be for more men of his strong, uncompromising type.

What a record he had as a preacher for 64 years! Has it ever been surpassed or even equalled? And he continued in harness to the very last. It had been evident for some months that his strength was failing, but he refused to give in. On Sunday he was present at both services in the Tabernacle, but it was his last public appearance. He remained in bed on Monday, and after a short, sharp heart attack on Tuesday he passed away early in the afternoon. It was perhaps as he would have wished that he died at his post. For him there was no long and weary waiting for the final summons; no season of inactivity to break down the eager spirit of one whose days had been so full of action. Quickly and quietly he passed from the ministries of earth to the wider ministries of heaven, where they serve Him day and night in His temple.

Mr. Findlay was a big man built on a big scale. This was true of him even physically. He would have arrested attention anywhere with his magnificent physique, and his tall, commanding presence. It seemed almost natural for him to be dominating and masterful. His very intimate friend, the late Dr. Duncan Main, of Hangchow, once said in his own witty way that he had "never known Pastor Findlay play second fiddle, but he had never known him blow his own trumpet." He was as autocratic in some of his ways as General Booth, and he had other qualities in common with the founder of the Salvation Army. He ruled his own congregation at the Tabernacle as Dr. Parker is said to have ruled his at the City Temple; reigning supreme over all its concerns; keeping everything in his own hands; and vesting the whole administration in a committee of one. In this age of dictators he was as near an approach to a spiritual dictator as we are ever likely to see.

For many years Pastor Findlay was himself the preacher at the Tabernacle services, but latterly he called to his aid preachers of all denominations and of none, from all parts of the Kingdom, for the Tabernacle stood on an independent basis owning no allegiance to any church, sect, or party. He also made it a rallying point for several of the independent missionary societies.

The Tabernacle must be judged by its fruits and these have been apparent to all. It is a very large building of its kind, with seating accommodation for about 1200. On special occasions it is often crowded to overflowing, but even at the regular Sunday services there are remarkable congregations. The complaint about declining church attendances has never applied to the Tabernacle. And it has proved a nursery of souls. Not at special seasons only, but almost all the year round it could be said of it, "This man and that man was born there." Then, in addition to being a great Evangelical centre, known all over this country, it has made its influence felt to the ends of the earth. It has sent out and maintained its "own missionaries" in many foreign fields, the pastor drawing nothing for his own support from the Tabernacle funds.

Mr. Findlay's other great interest in life was the work of the Orphan Homes of Scotland at Bridge-of-Weir. As the son-in-law of their founder, William Quarrier, he had a hereditary interest in the Homes and he was continuously associated with their administration from the very first until the day of his death. He was also accustomed to preside at the Wednesday evening church service and the Friday evening workers' meeting, and no figure was more familiar to the thousands of children who have passed through the Homes. It is fitting that this afternoon his mortal remains will find a place in the cemetery within the Orphan Home grounds beside the graves of Mr. and Mrs. Quarrier and other fellow-workers.

Amid all his activities Mr. Findlay found time to serve on several evangelical and missionary boards in Glasgow and London. He was always an untiring worker, persistently carrying out his methodical routine and labouring year after year, twelve hours a day for seven days a week. Concentration and consecration were two of the keynotes of his life. He concentrated with an inflexible purpose on what he felt to be his mission in life. Nothing was allowed to interfere with it. And his consecration was likewise wholehearted. In his youth he volunteered for the foreign mission field, but Hudson Taylor, the founder of the China Inland Mission, shrewdly said that he could render greater service at home in raising up other workers to go abroad. And that proved to be the case to an extent of which Hudson Taylor never dreamed.

There could never be any doubt about Mr. Findlay's theology. It did not change with the passing years. He was a man of one book—the Bible—which he implicitly believed from cover to cover. The results of the Higher Criticism left him unaffected;

the waves of modern thought swept around him in vain.   He stood
where he had always stood; holding to the last the faith of his
youth; proclaiming in old age the same Evangel as in his early days.
His beliefs admitted of no questioning, and there was never any
qualification in his preaching.

Not long ago an eminent theologian referred to the impression
made upon him by a preacher who was able, like a prophet of old,
to enforce all his message with "Thus saith the Lord."   "I felt,"
added this theologian of rather advanced views, " not only the
poverty of my own utterance in comparison, but that something
rich and strong had been lost to our age."   One of Mr. Findlay's
contributions to the age in which he lived and worked was just this
strong note of certainty.   He never failed to sound forth "Thus
saith the Lord," and therein perhaps lay a large part of the secret
of his power.

It is no figure of speech, but the actual truth, to say that we
"shall not look upon his like again."   Of Alexander Whyte it
was declared that "the mould was broken when God made him.
There can never be another after his pattern."   That is equally true
of Mr. Findlay.   He can have no successor of quite the same type.
But God fulfils Himself in many ways, and another race will arise,
using, perhaps, a new language in proclaiming the old Gospel to the
age in which their lot is cast.

Of Pastor Findlay it can truly be said he "served his own generation by the will of God," and he has "come to his grave in a full
age, like as a shock of corn cometh in in its season."   He fought a
good fight, he finished his course, he kept the faith.

June 18, 1938

XLIV

Dr. ARCHIBALD FLEMING

THERE was something pathetic and almost tragic in the close of the long and brilliant life of the Scotsman who had made his name so familiar everywhere as "Dr. Archibald Fleming of St. Columba's."

With a success acknowledged on all hands, Dr. Fleming had raised St. Columba's Church of Scotland to a position in London which was the envy even of the Church of England. On it he had lavished all the labour of the greater part of his lifetime, and he had the satisfaction of having made the name of St. Columba's almost a household word.

Then in a night air raid by the enemy over London, St. Columba's was destroyed, and Dr. Fleming was lying at Windsor so seriously ill that the news could not be broken to him. Perhaps it was better that he should never know how practically everything he had accomplished—at least outwardly—had been shattered at the last.

There was nothing in his earlier life that Archibald Fleming was more willing to recall than his association shortly after the close of his University course with W. E. Henley in the original *Scots Observer*. He contributed to the journal almost every week, and was one of a notable band of young writers which included Robert Louis Stevenson, J. M. Barrie, and others. He used to speak of the great days when a new poem of Rudyard Kipling's would come tumbling into the editor's room.

Fleming's assistantship in St. Cuthbert's, Edinburgh, was one of the formative periods of his career. It brought him into association with the famous Dr. James Macgregor, then at the height of his pulpit power, and the close relations then established were maintained until the end of Macgregor's life.

Ordained in 1888 as minister of the country parish of Newton, Midlothian, Fleming was called nine years later to the historic Tron Kirk in Edinburgh. It was during his ministry there that he was commanded, as a young minister in his twenties, to preach before Queen Victoria at Balmoral, and this proved to be almost a yearly visit until the close of Victoria's reign. He had reminiscences of meeting the Emperor of Germany and many members of the Royal

Family, and one afternoon he spent a merry time at the Crathie Church bazaar with a little girl who afterwards became Queen of Spain.

In 1902 Fleming went to St. Columba's Church of Scotland, Pont Street, London, with which his name was afterwards to be so closely linked. At that time St. Columba's was at a low ebb. Dr. Norman Maclean, who preached there in the first winter of the new ministry, has recalled that he said to himself: "Fleming has taken up a lost cause." Thirty years later he was glad to add that "the lost cause became a glorious victory."

Dr. Fleming from the very first had the dream of making "St. Columba's a great centre for all exiled Scots desiring to worship under the banner of that grand old church of our fathers, whose forms of worship we love and whose traditions we are proud to inherit." How greatly he succeeded became a matter of history. The membership rose in 30 years from 502 to over 2000, and the Christian liberality went up by leaps and bounds. Whilst it so largely devoted itself to the interests of Scots people, it became generous in helping wider causes. In the annual collection for London Hospitals St. Columba's year after year gave the largest sum of any congregation in the Metropolis—Church of England or Noncomformist.

Dr. Fleming established aristocratic connections in his ministry at St. Columba's. It must be admitted that he had a weakness for titles and social standing. Certainly he gathered around him a kirk-session such as could be matched nowhere else for the imposing array of names of peers and commoners, and leaders in the professional and business and literary life of the time. This, however, was in danger of being overdone; it was one of Dr. Fleming's peccadilloes.

Over against this, and by way of contrast, must be set the fact that on the roll of St. Columba's were the names of over 500 domestic servants. They were the special care of the deaconesses, working under Dr. Fleming, who also spent much of his time in serving the interests of the exiled Scots of all classes in London.

If ever any one had a fluent and facile pen it was Archibald Fleming. What he wrote at top speed had a grace of style which was coveted by his fellows. Even his sermons, which were always fully written out, were often hastily produced. I remember him once showing me where in the Athenæum Club he was accustomed to seek refuge from callers and interruptions in order to prepare his pulpit work. He was a habitue of the Athenæum,

Rev.
GEORGE GLADSTONE

Photo:
T. & R. ANNAN, Glasgow

Dr.
ARCHIBALD FLEMING

Photo:
VANDYK, London

Rev.
J. P. STRUTHERS

Principal
JAMES DENNEY

Photo:
T. & R. ANNAN, Glasgow

and would point out how near he sat to the Archbishop of Canterbury (Dr. Lang), and also where Mr. Baldwin (as he then was), would be almost lost in an armchair devouring a thriller.

But whenever and wherever his sermons were written, they bore not the slightest trace of rushed work.   They may have come hot from the anvil with all the glow still upon them, and in their form and style they were as perfect as if they were the fruit of long and laborious preparation.   They were unfailing in their grace of diction, with its fine delicacies of light and shade, and they were rich in imaginative power and cultured eloquence.   To the devotional part of his services he always gave special attention, and his pulpit prayers were often printed in response to private requests, while they were also prized by ministers as models for use in their churches.

Dr. Fleming was one of the pioneers in the new art of preaching on the wireless.   His first broadcast was in the first year of the B.B.C., and on a long succession of New Year Eves he preached over the wireless to multitudes of listeners.   In some ways he was at his best on the wireless.   His voice in the pulpit was sometimes weak and ineffective, but in broadcasting its tones were a perfect delight and the intimate touch of his addresses awoke many responsive chords.

On the day of Queen Alexandra's death Dr. Fleming was called away from a public dinner to broadcast a message from Savoy Hill and his almost extempore appreciation of the Queen Mother was a perfect bit of work.

A record was established by Dr. Fleming in the number of times he had been Chaplain to Moderators and Lord High Commissioners in the General Assembly of the Church of Scotland.   He was always perfectly at home in the Palace of Holyroodhouse, Edinburgh, and he had become so familiar with the whole routine that he was asked to undertake the codifying and printing of the unwritten laws regulating the relationships between the Lord High Commissioner and the Moderator.

It is no secret that he might have been Moderator of the General Assembly himself.   He had the offer of nomination in 1931, but felt it had to be a choice between the Moderatorship and St. Columba's, and he put St. Columba's first.

Thus he joined "the glorious company of the M.H.B.s" (the "Might Have Beens").   He coined the phrase and liked to use it.

July 5, 1941

XLV

Rev. GEORGE GLADSTONE

ORATORY is largely a lost art to-day, and one of the last of its great exponents in Glasgow was the Rev. George Gladstone. There must be many who can still hear echoes of his wonderful voice as he thrilled mass meetings in St. Andrew's Hall and elsewhere.

Minister of Dundas Street Church for 34 years, Gladstone was a leading personality in the Evangelical Union, and later in the larger Congregational Union of Scotland. By his brethren in the ministry he was greatly beloved, and in the churches throughout the denomination no man was held in greater honour.

But he was also an outstanding figure in the public life of Glasgow. In his day he was without a peer as a platform speaker. Particularly on behalf of the Temperance cause and Liberalism his utterances were not only powerful and telling in no ordinary degree, but memorable in the experience of many of his hearers.

On the political platform he had some extraordinary triumphs. St. Andrew's Hall was crowded with students to hear Lord Rosebery. At the close there were cries for "Gladstone." Lord Rosebery looked round in surprise and, after listening entranced to a brief speech, which roused the audience to enthusiasm, he rose and said: "I read in the evening papers that our leader, Mr. Gladstone, had left Euston Station to-day for one of his Midlothian campaigns, robed in a Highland mantle. As our friend spoke I could not but think that part of this eloquent mantle had fallen on his namesake, and whether he be related or not to the great Gladstone, our reverend friend has in a marked degree shared in the great gift of eloquent, stirring, and ennobling speech."

Of another scene, one who was present has written thus: "It is midsummer, 1886. The Prime Minister, Mr. Gladstone, addresses an immense gathering in Hengler's Circus, Glasgow. It is a day of sweltering heat, the large audience waiting for hours, oppressed and crowded. One or two of the speeches have really missed fire. The great master of speech and assemblies springs to his feet, brushing the chairman aside, and delivers one of his marvellous and inspiring speeches. Who can follow, since Demosthenes has spoken? There is a failure—let it be nameless. Then cries for 'Gladstone'! The Prime Minister looks round astonished. What means the cry? Must he speak again? A minute later and there stands at his side a tall, clerical-clad figure—easy, lithe, erect. There is a leaning of the head, just a little to the side, a moment's pause, then over that crowded, wearied audience break the mellow, flute-like notes and tones of that wonderful voice. They are held for a second time that day under a spell of eloquence, as Gladstone the second drives home in clear, manly, and thrilling words the lessons of the first speaker—the rights of men, of peoples, and of nations. A word of apology for having obtruded at such a meeting is met with admiring cries of 'Go on, George!' The speaker turns to go, but the elder Gladstone is on his feet, his eyes sparkle, an indication of how the lesser Gladstone's speech has met with his approval and appreciation. There is a hearty handshake, almost an embrace, and the two men go each their way, while the audience move out to the fresh air, and later to their homes by dale and vale and hill, by mountain, stream, and sea. Great is the power of speech. These two voices are stilled; we shall hear the silver-tongued speakers no more. Yet their words breathe a rich refreshment, they stir to action, and in their influence can never pass from the memory of man!"

These are but typical examples. Many more could be cited. for George Gladstone, to the end of his days, was the idol of popular audiences in Glasgow.

There was more than eloquence in his speaking. At its best it was pure oratory. He had a fine presence, with a lofty dignity; his beautiful, flexible voice was like a perfectly modulated musical instrument; and he had a power of dramatic delivery which came to him so easily as to seem perfectly natural.

To say that he had no such spectacular triumphs in the pulpit as on the platform is not to belittle his preaching. He held that preaching was the business of his life and he gloried in proclaiming the Gospel. There was no straining after popularity in his pulpit work. It was not for nothing that he had been the disciple and was the colleague and successor of that prince of expository preachers, Principal James Morison.

In the pulpit George Gladstone's aim ever seemed to be to reveal and to extol Jesus Christ, and the light on his face, and the tones of his voice as he came under the thrall of his theme, many remember to this day.

He took his preaching very seriously, in its preparation as well as in its delivery. His method with a text was to open up its hidden meaning and lay bare the thought of God enshrined in the Scriptures. In the pulpit he was always an ambassador, beseeching men to be reconciled to God. Very appropriately the text on his tombstone is "God forbid that I should glory, save in the Cross of our Lord Jesus Christ."

"The Cross," it was said, "was not a colouring matter brought in now and again to give a purple patch to his preaching, nor was it merely a pathetic incident narrated to give persuasiveness to an appeal. The Cross had become to him a method of thought, a temper, a habit of mind; it determined all his thinking, and formed the atmosphere through which he saw all things. The Cross pervaded his ministry because it possessed and fascinated his life. In the great congregation as in the small evangelistic gathering, in mission hall and in country church, he was equally at home in declaring the glory of the Cross."

One of his contemporaries, still in our midst, once described him in a phrase which any one might covet for an epitaph: "George Gladstone," he said, "was a white man through and through."

His death called forth striking public as well as private appreciations. It was then said of him:

> He held his place—
> Held on through blame and faltered not at praise.
> And when he fell, in whirlwind he went down,
> As when a kingly cedar, green with boughs,
> Goes down with a great shout upon the hills,
> And leaves a lonesome place against the sky.

November 15, 1941

XLVI

Principal JAMES DENNEY

OF all the men who have influenced Scottish preachers in this generation there is perhaps none to be compared with Dr. James Denney.

It is not only that students who sat on the benches of the Glasgow College in his time are for ever quoting "as Denney said" about this or that, but his spirit has entered into the whole warp and woof of their preaching, and of many others who came to know him only through his writings.

His influence has been on the matter rather than on the manner of preaching. Yet he was not insensible to the importance of the latter. He was a stickler for style, and like the eminent English Nonconformist, Dr. R. W. Dale, he had drilled himself in Burke. He knew his Shakespeare so well that he once declared that if the historical plays were lost he could reproduce them from memory. On a journey in Canada he read through the *Iliad* and "turned over" *Wilhelm Meister;* but *Wilhelm* had nothing to say to him: "I am only sorry I didn't put *Nicholas Nickleby* into my bag instead." Pepys, which he read twice, he thought the most interesting book that he knew: "There is not a square inch in it that has not interest, and it is as much a miracle in its way as *Othello.*" "It seems odd," he writes to a friend, "that I should lecture to a church society on two such blackguards as Gibbon and Cellini, but they are more interesting than Fathers, Reformation theologians, or modern divines."

In an article on "The Education of a Minister," which he once wrote in the London *Quarterly Review*, he spoke of the power, indispensable to a minister, "of putting his mind into language, clear, consecutive, and forcible. The loss the Gospel suffers because its ministers are insufficiently trained in this indispensable but difficult art—the art of expressing clearly and exactly their meaning—no words could tell." In the last paragraph he declared with emphasis that a wider and sounder knowledge of our own literature, and a power of self-expression owing something to it, "are of more value for the work of the ministry than much that we gain from what are considered distinctly professional studies,"

But it is in the content of the preaching of to-day that his influence has been felt most of all.   The great decision of his life was to preach the Atoning Death of the Lord Jesus Christ; to preach the Cross—on the one hand its power to save, and on the other its sharpness and sternness, its imperious calls to duty and self-denial.   And he sent out his students fired with something of his own resolve.

To see Denney himself in the pulpit was not to be immediately impressed.   Perhaps the first feeling was one of disappointment. There was nothing commanding, or even striking, in his appearance. An old student has remarked on the absence of anything prophetic or even leonine in the physical build of this great defender of the Faith.   One saw, instead, a tall, gaunt figure with pallid face, short grizzled beard and hair, and dark piercing eyes behind close-fitting spectacles.   Nor was his voice effective at the start.   Thin, high-pitched, and rather metallic in tone, it was only when he rose to a note of passion that it vibrated with thrilling effect.

When Denney left his church in Broughty Ferry for a Professor's Chair in Glasgow he burned all his sermons.   He continued, however, to preach incessantly, generally twice every Sunday.   For years he wrote none of his sermons, yet it was impossible to listen to him and find a sentence unfinished or any but the most fitting word used.   He had his defects in the pulpit. His wife, to whom he owed so much, complained of the lack of pathos in his preaching.   It was she who urged him: "Oh, James, keep down your hand in the pulpit and be gracious."   There was also a certain lack of colour in his sermons, and his disregard, and almost contempt, for the use of illustrations was a real weakness.

But for lucidity and directness and effectiveness in the presentation of a subject he was a master.   He used to say to his students: "Gentlemen, the first thing in a sermon is lucidity; the second is lucidity; and the third is lucidity."   What he preached to others in this respect he practised himself.   He had, it has been said, "a limpid clarity which glittered like a mountain stream."   Scholar as he was, he knew the necessity of adapting his message to the minds of his hearers.   His advice was: "Don't preach above people's heads; the man who shoots above the target does not prove thereby that he has superior ammunition.   He just proves that he can't shoot."   To the need for studying the structure of a sermon he was keenly alive.   Nothing better has been said about an effective conclusion than his advice: "Keep something of a gallop for the avenue."

It was characteristic of James Denney that, with all his love of learning, he once wrote to a friend: "It is my business to teach, but the one thing I covet to do is the work of an evangelist," and that he said more than once he "didn't care anything for a theology that didn't help a man to preach."

A young preacher, not of his own Church, said that while he "loved to sit at the feet of James Denney, he made one afraid to preach. He revealed not the preacher's art but his heart—a tremendous earnestness, a burning passion for Christ, an intense belief in the power of the Cross. I never forget his words: 'I had rather preach with a crucifix in my hand and the feeblest power of moral reflection than have the finest insight into ethical principles and no Son of God who came by blood'."

His theology helped him to preach and it made him the preacher he was. While always somewhat austere in the pulpit, his austerity was softened by the warm glow of his devotion to Jesus Christ, whose name in later years he could never utter without a quivering lip and a tremor in the voice. It was by his deeply reverent, yet calm, confident handling of the mysteries of the Faith that he "sent his hearers forth with uplifted head, taking to their souls the things that are for ever sure though the heavens should fall."

June 21, 1941

XLVII

Rev. J. P. STRUTHERS

FEW men with so great a distaste for fame ever became so famous as Struthers of Greenock. Principal James Denney said he was the only man of genius he was ever intimately acquainted with. The genius of Struthers became known to the world mainly through his little children's magazine, *The Morning Watch*, the like of which has not been seen before or since, and about which much could be said. But it is not merely as the "children's editor" that Struthers is still remembered to-day. As a minister he was distinguished in no ordinary way.

The main facts of his life can be briefly summarised. He was born in a humble home in Glasgow, became Dux of the High School, and carried off so many prizes in his last year that his father found it necessary to get a wheelbarrow to take them home. At the University his career was also one of the highest distinction; he was asked to offer himself as a candidate for the Snell Exhibition at Oxford, and had the offer of a Professorship of Greek in an Australian university. But he had decided to be a minister of the Reformed Presbyterian Church, one of the smallest denominations in Scotland, and nothing would deflect him from that purpose.

His first charge was at Whithorn, where he had three years of a happy ministry before he went to Greenock, which was destined to be the scene of his life work and which came to be inseparably associated with his name. Although at first he declined the call because of the claims of Whithorn, he frankly said: "I love Greenock, and would choose it of all places I know." And he never lost that love of Greenock through all the thirty-three years of his residence there.

His ministry was a success even in outward things, but he flatly refused to accept more than £200 of a salary! Mainly through his instrumentality a new church was built and the cost was cleared off on the opening day. The congregation was small but the church was alway full, as many people of other denominations attended. His week-night service attracted one of the most remarkable gatherings in the town. Those of us who were privileged to be at one of those week-night services found it a memorable experience.

In pastoral devotion Struthers was conspicuous. No detail was too small for his attention; no sacrifice of time or trouble was too great. Nor were his services confined to those who were his own members. All sorts and conditions of people came within his ambit. He would pick up drunkards from the streets, take them to his house, care for them till they sobered and then accompany them home. Over many of these he maintained a solicitous care. He had been known to visit some of them six times a week, and often three times a day. On one occasion, when he was leaving for a holiday, he received bad news of some of the poor folks in whom he was interested. Taking his travelling bag with him, he called on his way to the railway station, only to find the state of things worse even than he had expected. He was pressed to stay with them, and waited there for ten hours, with the result that he had to forego his holiday invitation.

Struthers was known to have carried a drunk woman, whom he found lying in a lonely place on the upper reaches of Greenock, to the shelter of the House of Refuge. To that institution and to Gateside Hospital he was a frequent visitor. Every week he took sweets for the children in hospital who were convalescent, and he had always a handful of cinnamon balls for the women at their washing tubs in the hospital laundry.

It was characteristic of Struthers, when he was visiting in the tenements and met women on the stairs with scuttles of coal, that he would insist on taking the scuttles from them and carrying them to their doors. Then there was the famous stone in his garden wall on the Esplanade, where he laid little bunches of flowers for any passer-by to take. "Daily," it was said, "and often several times a day, the fragrant sacrifice was laid upon the little stone altar, a share of the beauty of his garden, which he offered to whomsoever list to take it."

Struthers wrote out the main ideas of his sermons—usually seven pages—and he followed in general the lines of what he had written. But he never committed anything to memory. Then after 28 years' experience in the ministry he changed his method. Feeling that he was inclined to talk in a slipshod style, he decided to write out his sermons in full and read them from the pulpit.

Perhaps nothing better has ever been said of the preaching of Struthers than by the late Rev. Thomas Cassels in his delightful book "Men of the Knotted Heart," published many years ago. "I question," he said, "if in many generations there has been so unique an interpreter of the Bible. He brought to it a careful, exact scholarship, but other men have done that; he brought also a living zeal for the Gospel and the Kingdom, but so have other men; but he brought also an imagination which circled in a wide orbit round the poles of humour and austerity, and this was his unique gift.   Consequently, the Bible became in his hands a living thing, like Moses' rod.   It became a serpent to sting the conscience and arouse the soul.   He would take a text and turn it and combine it with others, and one would see in it deeps and gleams and beauties that few other preachers could reveal.   We have to go back to Thomas Fuller for a like holy wit and sanctified imagination."

The two outstanding peaks in the mountain range of his preaching were seen in expounding the Word and in declaring the love of God to men.   God's love was the first theme on which he preached as an ordained minister, and it was his last.   He had said in one of his letters: "I would like to die on a Sabbath day, or on a week-day after preaching.   I would like to be inviting sinners to come to God to the last hour of my life."

That wish was granted literally.   When preaching at the second service on Sunday, January 17th, 1915, from the text, "God, who giveth liberally," he was speaking on God's delight in giving when he suddenly fell on the pulpit floor and sank into unconsciousness, from which he only partially emerged at times until next morning, when he quietly passed away.

Tales will continue to be told of Struthers and his incorrigible humour, his quaint sayings, and his quixotic deeds, but what some will remember most of all will be how his heavy, sombre features were transfigured and his face became lustred with a strange light as he preached the love of God to men.

January 20, 1940

XLVIII

Dr. J. D. JONES

DR. J. D. JONES, of Bournemouth, was acknowledged to be the "Unmitred Bishop of Congregationalism" and an outstanding figure of his time in English Nonconformity.

But he was also well known in Scotland, and was a frequent visitor north of the Tweed. I met him personally when he was at the zenith of his power, and I had often heard him in the pulpit and on the public platform.

"J. D.," as he was familiarly known everywhere, was an ecclesiastical statesman of the first rank. All that he did for Congregationalism as a denomination it would be impossible to estimate. It was mainly through his efforts and influence that the Congregationalists were led to see that, while Independency had its merits, there was also something to be said for linking the churches together in mutual interest and helpfulness. For many years his hand controlled most of the machinery. He was the John White of Congregationalism.

Dr. Jones was successful in raising over £750,000 for the Congregational churches, and Mr. Lloyd George once said that, had he been a politician, he would have "persuaded people to pay income tax without knowing they were doing it."

But to the general public outside Congregational circles he was best known as a preacher. He was not one of our greatest preachers. His sermons were not particularly outstanding either in intellectual brilliance or in surpassing eloquence of delivery. But he had a pulpit influence of peculiar power. For nearly forty years in Bournemouth he attracted crowded congregations, which included Anglicans as well as Protestants of all shades, and wherever he preached throughout the Kingdom people flocked to hear him.

His success in Bournemouth can always be cited as one of the strongest arguments in favour of long-term ministries. For nearly forty years his pulpit popularity remained undiminished. Richmond Hill Church was the Mecca of worshippers from all denominations. Anglicans were always to be found in large numbers in what the little girl said was the church of "St. Jones's." The crowds were there the whole year round, but in the holiday season the "professional packers" were faced with an impossible task and many people had to be turned away.

There was nothing very profound in the preaching of Dr. Jones; there was certainly nothing sensational. His pulpit gifts were not of a startling or turbulent order. He reminded one of Dr. G. H. Morrison in a simplicity which was so deceptive as to conceal the art behind it all. It was truly said that "perhaps only one in fifty had any adequate or educated idea of the preacher's consummate technique and homiletic mastery; the remaining forty-nine were attracted by the note of quiet strength and comfort which ran through all his utterances."

Dr. Jones was essentially a comforting preacher. He did not worry tired, harassed people with problems, nor confront them with great public issues which perhaps affected them but little. He addressed himself to the personal private needs of individuals; he brought them the consolation which not only wiped away their tears, but gave them a new sense of strength. And that largely explained his popularity in an age when men and women, bewildered as well as baffled, were crying out, as perhaps never before, for a sure word from the pulpit.

One can understand Mr. Ernest H. Jeffs when he said: "The thought of music arises inevitably as one thinks of J. D. Jones' preaching. More than once, after sitting in denominational Assemblies and listening to the dull or harsh prose of debate, I have gone to hear J. D. Jones preach merely for the pleasure of sitting back and resting in the smooth and gracious melody!"

Not only were his sermons most carefully written, but he took his manuscript to the pulpit, and always used it. He read his sermons, and read them in a way that made it almost impossible for his hearers to realise that he was reading.

Where, then, it may be asked, was the secret of his power as a preacher? The best description I have seen was by his great friend Silvester Horne, who wrote: "His style is supremely artless. That is where 'J. D.' is unique. 'Let us take this pleasant country walk,' he seems to say, and because you cannot possibly refuse his winning invitation you go with him, and you feel your feet are across the frontier of the Divine Kingdom before you realise where you are."

It is good to know that, while thus devoting himself to his pulpit work and spending so much time in committees and on denominational affairs, Dr. Jones was at the same time a true pastor. "He knew his people by name, and he radiated geniality on his way.

He carried their burdens on his own heart; no bed of sickness lacked the balm of his healing presence, no infirm or aged member was left forlorn or bereft of words of solace. Those who had anxieties about business, or were distressed by fortune, found in their minister not merely a sympathetic ear but practical help."

A lady member of his congregation put it all in an epigram when she said that "he made sad family occasions beautiful, and happy ones happier."

Ecclesiastic and man of affairs as he was to the finger-tips, nothing would ever tempt Dr. Jones away from what he regarded as the great work of his life. He was once asked by the leader of one of the political parties whether he would consent to be a Parliamentary candidate, and he was offered the choice of constituencies. He wrote back a letter of thanks begging to be forgiven if he answered in a word of Scripture. The Scripture word he quoted was the answer Nehemiah gave to Sanballat and Tobiah when they tried to tempt him away from his work of building the wall of Jerusalem: "I am doing a great work so that I cannot come down." Dr. Jones, in telling the incident, says he underlined those last two words. "It would have been a 'come down' to forsake the pulpit for the political arena. I do not disparage the work that Parliament can do in the way of bettering human conditions, but the ultimate healing of the world's hurt is not to be effected by legislation but by the redeeming grace of God, and the proclamation of that redeeming grace is the highest work to which any man can be called. So that, as I look back, I am humbly grateful to God, that He called me into the holy ministry."

It is fitting that on his tombstone he is described simply as "Preacher of the Gospel."

April 25, 1942

XLIX

Rev. T. N. TATTERSALL

THE news of the sudden death of Rev. T. N. Tattersall came as a shock, and it has called forth many expressions of profound regret.

At Easter last year Mr. Tattersall had some slight heart attacks and had been advised to go slowly. In October, after examination by specialists, this warning was repeated. But he continued to preach, and when preaching it was impossible for him to take it easy. He was not built that way.

Still he carried on until recently when there came a very serious heart attack. This was followed by another a week later, and in little over half an hour all was over. He had been out of his pulpit only three Sundays and in his church magazine for this month he wrote that he hoped to be preaching again to-morrow, 14th instant.

After a funeral service in his church at Purley on Friday of last week his mortal remains were taken to the Greenlawn Memorial Park, Warlingham, a peaceful country spot to which he had been greatly attracted. His grave in the lawn is surrounded by beds of shrubs and flowers, a fitting last resting-place for one whose soul was attuned to beauty and responsive to all that was lovely in life.

Thus at the age of 63, when years of work and usefulness might still have seemed to lie in front of him, there passed away a gifted and radiant spirit who greatly enriched the lives of all who were brought into contact with him. As Robertson Nicoll said of one whose preaching and personality made a deep impression in a former generation, there may be said with equal truth of T. N. Tattersall: "He did not know how to take care of himself, and so to-day many people in many places mourn and miss him, and will continue to miss him all the time between the digging of his grave and theirs."

The deepest sympathy goes out to Mrs. Tattersall, the angel of his home these many years, and her two married daughters, one beside her in London and the other in Canada. The only son of the family, a brilliant young man of high promise, on whom many hopes were centred, met his death in an accident shortly after joining the Forces in Canada to serve in the present war.

More than twenty years have passed since I first heard Mr. Tattersall. He was then entirely unknown to me except by name. Then one evening he spoke at a meeting at which I was present, and what I heard made me anxious to hear more. The next Sunday I made my way to his church—Adelaide Place Baptist—and there again I found it to be an experience and an adventure to listen to him. My first impression of him as a preacher of remarkable power has only been confirmed and strengthened the longer and the better I knew him.

His subject that Sunday evening was "Jesus Christ and the Working Man," and the theme so permeated the whole service as to give it that unity which is so desirable and so helpful. It was felt in the Scripture Lesson which was read as he only could read it. He could give almost any passage a new and impressive meaning. I know people who would have gone far to hear him read the 55th chapter of Isaiah. He knew it so well that it was scarcely necessary for him to glance at the page in front of him, and as he read the glowing words in that rare voice so capable of every inflexion of tone, his fine face became irradiated, and his hearers caught something of the thrill. It was not an elocutionary effect—the reading was greater and the effect deeper than any mere elocution could ever produce.

The unity of the service was also maintained in the prayers. "Thou knowest how worried and anxious and careworn are many of the sons of men." "We pray for the men with empty hands and empty pockets, eyes without hope, the hearth without fire, and the cupboard so bare."

Mr. Tattersall showed the art of arresting attention in the striking opening passage of his sermon. The interest was never allowed to flag. There were apt and up-to-date allusions and telling illustrations. While insisting on the dignity of work and the fact that toil was good for a man, he said it was not good for him so to toil that "on his face was the emptiness of the ages, and on his back was the burden of the world." The existing social conditions he regarded as inimical to the religious life of many, and yet, the more difficult their lot, the more would they find their need of religion—a need only to be met and satisfied in Jesus Christ. He closed with a passionate and moving appeal for allegiance to the Lord of Glory, "Who wore the robe of a peasant and had the horny hands of a man of toil."

Unfortunately Mr. Tattersall remained in Glasgow only for a few years, but it was amazing how abiding was the impression he made in that short time. Friendships then formed followed him in his subsequent ministries in Swansea, Toronto, Edinburgh, and Purley, and he had a great welcome on his return visits to the city and its neighbourhood.

In the war of 1914-1918 Mr. Tattersall served as a Chaplain with the Forces at the Front, influencing the men with his selfless devotion, and displaying such bravery as won for him the award of the D.S.O. He was anxious to serve again in this war, and made an effort to return as a Chaplain but he was rejected on medical grounds. Characteristically he sought another outlet for his zeal, and he gave several terms of service with the Y.M.C.A. Huts and Canteens in this country.

It is no exaggeration, but only the simple truth, to say that T. N. Tattersall was a man of beautiful character and lovable personality. There was nothing in the least sanctimonious about him; anything in the form of religiosity was foreign to his nature. He was human, genial, humorous, with his genuine goodness always shining through and a sincerity that was as transparent as the day.

And what a preacher he was when at his best. Acutely sensitive and very susceptible to atmosphere, he could rise to remarkable heights when he was in his right environment. His glorious voice, the voice of an orator, deep and resonant, could flare forth like a trombone or be as soft as a whisper.

There was true art in his preaching, but there was far more than that. He had strong convictions, which he was fearless in proclaiming. How he could stir a crowded audience in St. Andrew's Hall! His preaching had power and passion, but it had likewise a gentle winsome note. While he could sound a bugle call to youth, he had also a message for the old and weary, the bruised and broken.

> *Hail and farewell. The laurels with the dust*
> *Are levelled, but thou hast thy surer crown,*
> *Peace, and immortal calm, the victory won.*
> *Somewhere serene thy watchful power inspires;*
> *Thou art a living purpose, being dead,*
> *A fruit of nobleness in lesser lives.*
> *A guardian and a guide; hail and farewell.*

March 13, 1943

L

Rev. W. H. LAX

TO those who never knew Rev. W. H. Lax it is difficult to convey any idea as to the manner of man he was. He had a personality of singular fascination which wove its spell over all manner of people.

When, as Mayor of Poplar, he attended a garden party at Buckingham Palace and was presented to King George V, the conversation was so interesting that his Majesty was moved to remark with a smile: "Why, Mr. Mayor, you will soon persuade me to be a Methodist!" It was the same with the costers and the charwomen of Poplar—he won them in the most artless way.

It was my privilege to hear Lax on various occasions and to be brought into personal contact with him. Some men who seem great in the pulpit and on the public platform are neither so impressive nor so attractive when one meets them in private. That was not my experience with Lax. He was quite unspoiled by fame; utterly unaffected in his bearing; a delightful conversationalist and a raconteur with a humour bubbling up spontaneously; and there was always about him a ring of sterling sincerity. The firm, eager clasp of his hand, the tones of his voice—these one can never forget.

His first sermon was preached when he was only 17 years of age, and he broke down after ten minutes. It was amusing to hear him telling of how his uncle afterwards admonished him, saying: "Never break down, lad; keep on talking—talk nonsense, if need be—but *never break down*."

Both in public and in private he could tell some delightful stories of his Poplar people. When one of them, a coster, was ill with a severe attack of laryngitis he called to see him. The man himself was hardly able to speak when Lax expressed his sympathy. But Billy's wife replied for him. "Thank ye, sir," she said, "I knowed ye'd be sorry, 'cos yer like Billy; yer both earn yer livin' with 'ollerin'."

When Lax's mother died, Poplar had a wonderful opportunity for showing sympathy. The people showered their kindly remarks on him as he went along the streets. Sometimes it was quaintly expressed sympathy: "Yer lookin' sad, sir," said one old lady. "I am feeling sad, Mrs. Bindle," explained the minister. "I have just heard that my mother has gone to heaven." "Well, don't worry, Mr. Lax," she replied in the kindest of tones, as she put her hand on his shoulder, "per'aps she 'asn't."

It was no wonder that his church came to be popularly known as "Lax's." The Rector of Poplar once stopped him in the street and humorously put to him an ecclesiastical problem. He said "The Church of England I know; the Congregational Church I know; the Presbyterian Church I know; the Baptist Church I know, but what is 'Lax's Church'?"

Lax never used a pulpit gown, but when preaching or lecturing he discarded his usual coat or jacket for a long, thin, black alpaca coat. This, I found, was because in speaking he always became wet with perspiration. He had usually to change clothes after a service.

What a speaker this little man was! He may not have been a great preacher in the sense in which that term is often understood. Certainly he himself would have been the last to claim such a title. But for sheer power over an audience he was fit to rank with the greatest. There are only two speakers with whom I would have compared him for that wizardry of eloquence which so completely captivates an audience. One is Lloyd George, whom I have seen when he was at the height of his power on the platform, doing what he willed with a crowd. The other was John McNeill, who was as Scottish as Lax was English, but had the same power of pathos and humour and the same irresistible sway over his hearers.

Lax, it has been truly said, was a born actor. What a success he would have been on the stage! Every movement was eloquent. He spoke not only with his voice but with his hands. I cannot recall any speaker who could use his hands so expressively. There was artistry in every turn and it all came to him as naturally as breathing. He proclaimed the Evangel—for he was Evangelical to the core—with a wooing and winning note, and he could draw on his own unrivalled experience for examples of brands plucked from the burning, of lives restored and made radiant under the influence of the Gospel.

In an age when public lecturing was almost a lost art, Lax continued to demonstrate its great possibilities. On the platform he found vent for all his dramatic power. With his ready and at times rollicking humour, and his tender pathos, he had his hearers laughing at one moment and weeping the next. They were for the time being as clay in the hands of the potter. In character-isation he excelled. The characters he created with verbal imagery he also personated with lifelike fidelity. I have seen him keep a Glasgow audience spellbound and entirely oblivious of time for as long as he cared to speak.

Wherever he went, up and down the country—and Lax travelled thousands of miles every year—crowds flocked to hear him. Yet he never failed to keep a close personal touch with his own people in Poplar. Great in his power as a popular preacher, he was equally great in his influence as a pastor—a very rare combination.

He was indeed the ideal pastor, sharing in all the joys and sorrows of his people. They ran instinctively to him in their need, and they never went in vain. By night as well as day he was ready to respond to any call. He sat at their firesides, sharing their humble meals, often at considerable personal risk, and all the time gave them the impression he was at a royal banquet. He received the most intimate confidences of all sorts and conditions of men and women; the forsaken and the broken poured out their hearts to him. Many a sad story he heard, and many a life he rescued from ruin by persistent, persuasive, and gallant personal service and sacrifice.

It was because "little Lax" was so big-hearted that he acquired so great an influence. Although he attracted the crowds, he spent his time and strength caring for individual men and women. With all his shining gifts of dramatic eloquence, if he had been less the pastor he would not have been so much the preacher.

February 20, 1943

LI

Dr. JOHN WATSON

IT was not until Rev. Dr. John Watson had become known as "Ian Maclaren" that he blossomed into fame as a preacher.

In Liverpool he had established a great reputation as minister of Sefton Park Presbyterian Church and was a leading pulpit force in the community. But the reputation was largely a local one. It was on the publication of "The Bonnie Brier Bush," his first collection of stories in the Kailyard school of fiction, that he suddenly burst into a startling popularity. Sentimental these stories undoubtedly were—they made even the critics cry—but they had humour as well as pathos.

It was his avowed end and aim to bring out the idyllic element in life, and he thus helped to slake the eternal thirst of human nature for those waters of the ideal that glimmer before us.

Since edition after edition of his first and succeeding volumes of Scots idylls came from the press until their circulation in this country and America ran into many hundreds of thousands, he found that when he appeared in any pulpit throughout the land there were crowds flocking to hear him.

Yet, the fact remains that when he was at his best he was a preacher of no ordinary gifts. Perhaps he was least successful during his three years' Glasgow ministry in St. Matthew's Church, Charing Cross. One elder said of him, "Ah, weel, a nice enough young man, but there's nae future in his heid." Another, in bidding him good-bye, shook him warmly by the hand, saying: "Well, Mr. Watson, I wish you all success. You may be a pastor, but you'll never be a preacher."

The circumstances in Glasgow were uncongenial, but after he went to Liverpool his gifts began to flower in the happy atmosphere of Sefton Park Church, an atmosphere which was very much of his own making. Year by year his development was continuous until he reached the height of his powers. His natural endowments were considerable. He had a resonant voice capable of many inflexions, while his tall and commanding figure arrested attention. An occasional lift of the hand was almost his only gesture, but his power of facial expression could rivet his hearers.

Dr.
J. D. JONES

Photo:
VANDYK, London

Rev.
T. N. TATTERSALL

To face page 176

Rev.
W. H. LAX

Photo:
WHIFFIN, Poplar

Dr.
JOHN WATSON

Photo:
NOREEN KIRBY, Liverpool

No man of his time could make a more effective appearance on great public occasions. His oratorical power was then most in evidence, yet I never thought he was at his best as a preacher on such occasions. His finest sermons were preached at ordinary services. In his own pulpit he maintained a consistently high standard Sunday after Sunday.

One of his members has left this testimony: "Dr. Watson's preaching was extempore in effect, for though a manuscript was always before him for reference, a quick turn of the leaves now and again was the only sign of its presence. He never read, yet as the following anecdote will show, his memory was wonderfully accurate. His sermons were so original and striking that it was impossible to forget them, yet he bravely repeated several of their number from time to time: sometimes at the request of a member of the congregation, always, I think, to the pleasure of his hearers. My own memory, sadly deficient in some directions, is tenacious of words, and in listening to these repeated sermons I used to wait in a sort of tremor to hear whether at certain telling passages, the right word would come in the right place. I once said to him: 'I knew that that illustration about the pool was coming, and waited to see if you would call it "the sullen pool," as you did before. If you had said "the turgid pool" or "the muddy pool," I think I should almost have been obliged to correct you.' He asked eagerly, 'And did I say "sullen"?' and on receiving an affirmative answer, 'That's very interesting,' he said, 'very interesting. I did not know I repeated myself so accurately. I suppose the original idea was so vivid, that it remains imprinted in my mind'."

Has ever anything more striking been told about old sermons than this? "One Sunday evening," says this hearer—"as a very rare exception I elected to stay at home—and on my sister's return from church I questioned her about the service. She looked at me in a sympathetic manner and said quietly, 'Dr. Watson preached on "The Peace of God." ' I had heard that sermon twice before, but after all those years the intense disappointment of that moment remains with me. The opportunity of hearing that most beautiful message a third time had been mine, and I had wilfully thrown it away. I could not forgive myself, and the entire family condoled with me in my loss." And the hearer adds, "Of how many preachers could such an incident be recorded?"

In spite of his facility in the use of language, Dr. Watson came to think that he had spent too little time on the form of his sermons. In himself he was an example of steady toil in

12

preparation. The want of distinction in the case of a speaker dealing with the most majestic ideas he thought a crime. "It is," he said, "a species of profanity. It is an act of intellectual indecency." He declared that if he had to begin again he would seek more earnestly a becoming dress for the message of God, and he thought the time would come when the preacher would be held responsible not only for the truth which he declared, but for the dress in which he clothed it.

Yet a member of his congregation said he had only once heard him preach a poor sermon. He was more than surprised when the preacher faltered time and again, but later on it was learned that he had sat by the bedside of a dying elder of his church throughout the whole of Saturday night, and had gone straight to his pulpit worn out and depressed. Incidentally, this throws a light on a pastoral fidelity which was conspicuous throughout his whole ministry.

There has often been quoted John Watson's dictum that the chief end of preaching was comfort. "Be pitiful," he used to say, "for every one is fighting a hard battle." In sermons on Biblical criticism and philosophy he had no faith whatever and in this connection he related an interesting personal experience.

"When I have in my day, like us all, attempted to reconcile science and religion, one of the greatest men of science, who used to be a hearer in my church, never seemed to be interested, but when I dealt with the deep affairs of the soul, he would come round in the afternoon to talk it out."

This saying of his also is self-revealing. "I now clearly see that every sentence should suggest Christ, and every sermon, even though His name had not been mentioned, nor His words quoted, should leave the hearer at the feet of Christ."

It could not be claimed that John Watson was in the front rank of great preachers; that he was one of the princes of the pulpit like Spurgeon or Parker or Liddon. But he had great gifts which stood the test of many years in the practical work of the ministry. A distinguished scholar who was among his regular hearers once said to him: "Your best work in the pulpit has been to put heart into men for the coming week."

November 13, 1943

LII

Dr. GEORGE H. MORRISON

IT used to be said that just as visitors to London in bygone days felt that they must of necessity hear Spurgeon or Parker or Liddon, so visitors to Glasgow in more recent years had the feeling that they could not miss hearing Dr. George H. Morrison in Wellington Church. One of the most noted of English Bishops, after fulfilling an afternoon engagement at the University, hurried off to be in time for the evening service at Wellington. And the miner from Fifeshire, or the crofter from the Hebrides, spending a Sunday in Glasgow, would have considered the day incomplete if they did not hear Dr. Morrison.

To Glasgow Dr. Morrison's ministry at Wellington was something like what Dr. Alexander Whyte's ministry at St. George's was to Edinburgh. Different in many ways, they were alike in the extent to which they captured the community and maintained their unbroken hold year after year.

Dr. Morrison was a great preacher who was also a great pastor. Of this rather unusual combination he was, indeed, the supreme example.

His genius as a preacher was never more clearly shown than by his success in solving the problem of the second service. Shortly after his settlement in Glasgow, the afternoon service was giving place to an evening one, but the results in general were not too satisfactory. When Wellington decided on an evening service Dr. Morrison was determined to give it a distinctive character. In the mornings he adhered to the old Scottish tradition of expository preaching.

In the evenings he allowed himself a wider scope, presenting the Christian essentials in a somewhat different setting, and, as he said, calling to his help every type of illustrative aid that appealed to him. He strove to give these evening addresses a strong human interest, in order, as he put it, "to win the attention, in honourable ways, of some at least of the vast class of people who sit very loosely to the Church. The touch is naturally far lighter than in the morning, but this does not mean lack of preparation. I prepare as carefully for the one as for the other." His one aim in preaching, he once said, was "to help people along the road." Here I may interpolate how Dr. Morrison once told me that, after he had fully prepared his subject, he set himself the task of striving to see how simply he could present it. His simplicity, therefore, was not the easy, facile thing some may have supposed it to be; it was the fruit of definite and earnest effort.

The response at his evening service was immediate and striking. The church became crowded to overflowing, long queues formed in University Avenue before the doors were opened and this was no mere passing phase. The same state of matters continued for over 26 years, right to the end of his ministry. And he got the class of people he set out to reach. These crowded evening congregations at Wellington made an interesting study in themselves. All classes and all ages were represented, but young men and women were always largely in evidence. Nor were they there because of the prospect of any novelty or sensation. They could only have been drawn because they felt that their wistful longings and inarticulate yearnings were somehow met and answered by the man in the pulpit with the soft voice, the quiet effortless style, and the subtle elusive charm.

There was no clangorous or challenging presentation of a new Evangel. Dr. Morrison's secret was in taking old familiar truths and clothing them in fresh robes of language which made them sparkle with a lustre of their own and revealed meanings hitherto hidden and unsuspected. He had a perfect flair in the selection of texts often fresh and suggestive. "He gave them drink out of the depths", "In the day that thou stoodest on the other side", "The deep that croucheth beneath", "Thou didst cleave the earth with rivers," are some that may be quoted, almost at random.

Many of his sermons were prose poems; all of them were suffused with a tender charm and rich in spiritual helpfulness. Volume after volume was published, and G. H. Morrison's sermons found a place in manse libraries everywhere, almost like those of F. W. Robertson, of Brighton, while they also very markedly appealed to a wide circle of lay readers. They revealed him to be both a mystic and a man of letters, and were acknowledged to place him in the foremost ranks of British preachers.

One fact of historic interest which should be mentioned is that it fell to Dr. Morrison to preach the first sermon on the wireless in Scotland. It was on the afternoon of Sunday, January 28, 1923, and it went forth from a temporary broadcasting station at Kelvinside, Glasgow. There was widespread public interest. It was

my privilege to be with the preacher and the operator in the little
inner room on that memorable occasion.   I remember how Dr.
Morrison, without using a single note, was able with his unerring
instinct, to finish exactly on the stroke of time.   Nor was it a case
of making some disjointed remarks, or of cutting down at the close.
It was a clear-cut, cameo-like sermon of ten minutes on the text,
"Above all taking the shield of faith."

There are many people who still remember this or that sermon
of Dr. Morrison's; there are as many who love to recall instances
of his pastoral devotion.   His routine visitation, so extensive and
incessant, was but one feature of his pastoral activity.   Many tales
could be told of his constant solicitous care of the sick and those in
sorrow or trouble.   And no success or joy that came to any member
of any family in his congregation was overlooked or allowed to pass
without letters or post-cards from him, which are still prized
possessions.

The end of this notable ministry came swiftly and unexpectedly
when Dr. Morrison was at the age of 62, and while there was no
sign of any waning of his powers and no abatement of his popularity.
In the first week of October, 1928, he was back from his summer
holiday—he held that a good holiday was a *sine qua non* for a minister
—and he was getting into the full stream of another winter's activities.   On the Wednesday afternoon he had spent three continuous
hours in the homes of his people, and in the evening he gave a
memorable address to a small company of workers in the hall of
Gorbals Church.   On Thursday evening he became seriously ill,
and on Sunday morning shortly after midnight he passed away,
almost before his illness had become generally known.

On the day before he died, when there was a slight rally, he was
able to have in his hands one of the early copies of a book to which
he had been looking forward—his biography, which I had written at
the request of London publishers, and in the preparation of which
he had given me every facility with his characteristic kindness.

Although Dr. Morrison did not reach the allotted span, he, if
any man, had done what he used to call "a good day's darg."   He
warned young preachers against unprofitable bustle and rush, and
preoccupation with small affairs and trifling engagements.   A
master of method, he so ordered his time that, while he was never
idle, he was never hurried or flurried.   There was always about him
a calm serenity, and as he moved among men he seemed a living
epistle of what he preached.

August 26, 1944

LIII

Principal W. M. MACGREGOR

IN the death of Emeritus-Principal W. M. Macgregor there has passed away one of the great figures in the Church life of our time. He was great in his intellect, in his preaching power, and in his personality. No man was further removed from the commonplace. In face and figure, in the tones of his voice, and in the pungency of his speech he was in a class all by himself.

"W.M.", as he was familiarly known, was never a popular preacher in the usual sense of that term. Neither in Renfield Church, Glasgow, nor in St. Andrew's, Edinburgh, where he was in the heyday of his strength, did he ever attract the crowd. He once said: "We all, on occasion, must have seen a preacher starting off in a blaze of passion before his people were well settled in their pews, and it has looked like nothing in the world but a railway engine snorting away before it has been coupled to its train. There was noise and energy enough for anything, but the passengers stayed where they were."

That was not his way. In his sermons he moved with a masterly and stately step, with an unhurried ease, and the lucidity and simplicity of his style never concealed the profound ability behind it all. He was pre-eminently a preacher to preachers, and his published volumes of sermons, so penetrating and piercing, so rich and mellow and truly spiritual in their teaching, are among those sure to endure.

In conversation, W. M. Macgregor struck off many a pregnant phrase with effortless ease, and a collection of his *obiter dicta* would make a priceless volume. He could be scathing in his criticisms, for he did not mince his words. On occasion he could become deliberately and charmingly sesquipedalian, as when he once declared: "It takes an extraordinary concatenation of meteorological circumstances (every syllable of every word being lovingly and lengthily pronounced) to make it possible for some people to go to church."

With his Dante-esque profile and what seemed often a severe and forbidding countenance, W. M. Macgregor had a kind heart, and many stories could be told of how he went out of his way to

help his old students.   He was also very appreciative of earnest
and sincere work, although he could use whips and scorpions when
he felt moved to scorn.   Fame and success had no effect on him;
an austere simplicity marked his whole habit of life.

No one was readier to respond to preaching invitations than Dr.
Macgregor.   Wherever he went he gave of his best.   Many a
congregation has treasured memories of his preaching.   Even his
peculiarities of voice are treasured, especially his characteristic
tendency to linger on the "a" in substantives ending with "ation."

One thing many will recall was the way he used to go round
hearing the preaching of his old students after they were settled in
charges of their own.   He drifted into churches unannounced and
took his place quietly among the congregation.   It was a severe
ordeal for those who had sat under him in the Divinity Hall; who
knew his very high and exacting standards, and who, perhaps, remembered that, long years before they knew him, he had been
declared to be preaching sermons superior to those of Chalmers
and Guthrie.   He was a curious and somewhat baffling hearer.   He
might sit hunched up in the pew and seldom seeming to see the
preacher in the pulpit.   But he missed nothing, and it was a great
gratification to him when afterwards he could speak words of real
encouragement in the vestry.

At the celebration of his jubilee Dr. Macgregor said that looking
back he could mark his ministry by three main stages.   The first
unquestionably in its influence upon his whole life was the coming
of Moody in the early 'seventies, when there was that surging deep
emotion all through the land.   The next stage was his entering
what was then the Free Church College, Glasgow.   The third
stage, after he left the Divinity Hall, which greatly influenced him,
was his going into the ministry.   There he learned more than any
teachers could have taught him.   The younger men, he said, had
got to learn that a village was an infinitely more interesting place
to work in than a town.   A city was a dull place with uniform
people who had their edges and corners rubbed off.

In course of his speech on this occasion Dr. Macgregor mentioned an interesting fact.   He recalled that during his Glasgow
ministry—from 1890 to 1898—he taught his friend, James Moffatt,
the New Testament.

Two specially happy memories of his later years may be recalled.
One was his address at the unveiling of a memorial to Principal
James Denney.   There he was in his best and most characteristic
form.   Who could ever forget how he spoke of Denney as having

"the most admirable gift of pregnant and witty and often demoralising utterance." True as it was of Denney, it was felt by every one that it was none the less true of Macgregor himself. Equally pointed was his remark that, while Denney had a small circle of devoted friends, "the majority of us would have declared of him what Emerson said of Thoreau: 'I would no more think of taking his arm than of taking the arm of an elm tree!'" And with what infinite relish he quoted the remark of Denney about a certain energetic and locquacious minister that "he had a really notable gift for the clamorous presentation of the obvious."

The other occasion gave him great personal gratification. It was when he delivered in Glasgow his course of lectures under the Preachers' Lectureship. The attendances, large from the first, steadily grew throughout the week until they were really remarkable. For an octogenarian who had to travel from Edinburgh daily and face a crowded audience of students and ministers it was no mean physical feat, but what made every one marvel was the intellectual power of this Emeritus-Principal, who had come out of his retirement to speak on the subject of preaching on which he had long been an acknowledged master, and who had lost none of his penetrating insight, his pungency of phrase, or his unique power of appeal. Dr. Macgregor himself was manifestly moved by the response he received; it seemed like the crown of his life-work.

Although he had reached the age of 83, he retained his erect and noble bearing, and he was still active. He had promised to preach in his old pulpit in St. Andrew's, Drumsheugh Gardens, on Sunday, and he had other engagements in his book. The last thing he wrote was an appreciation of his friend and former colleague the late Professor James Moffatt, and he had gone with it to the post when he was seized with illness. After three days in bed, with almost no suffering, he passed away peacefully in his sleep.

Principal Macgregor was so distinctive in personality and gifts that he cannot be forgotten. No one was more often the subject of conversation. His appearance was arresting and fascinating; his words were always memorable.

July 15, 1944

LIV

Dr. F. L. WISEMAN

A GREAT pillar of the Church has fallen in the death of Dr. F. L. Wiseman. He was within a fortnight of his 88th birthday, but he had preached twice on Sunday, and after returning to his home he fell asleep in his chair, and it proved to be his last long sleep.

Known and honoured in all the Churches, Dr. Wiseman was one of the greatest Methodists of his time. He had been twice President of the Conference, and had received every honour that Methodism had to bestow. And he served Methodism as few have ever done. It is unnecessary to recall how, even as an octogenarian, he was equal to its every emergency. It seemed to turn instinctively to him and he never failed it.

When Dr. Dinsdale T. Young died and left the great preaching centre at Westminster vacant, it was Dr. Wiseman who stepped into the breach and maintained the vast congregations until a successor was settled. And when the historic Wesley's Chapel in City Road was in a difficulty, it was, of course, Dr. Wiseman again who came to the rescue. There was surely something very fitting in the fact that the last sermons on the last day of the life of this famous follower of Wesley were preached from Wesley's pulpit.

Even princes of the pulpit are not always at their best, and Dr. Wiseman was no exception. But when he was at his best, he was certainly supreme in a way that was all his own. I have heard him on some of the days when he swept everything before him. In its range and grasp, in its passion and abandon, in its dramatic force and power, it was preaching on the grand scale such as we seldom get to-day. There was eloquence in it and there was oratory, and all the time it was real Gospel preaching. Quite recently this advice was given to young people: "If you have the opportunity of hearing Wiseman preach—and sing—don't miss it. It will be something to talk of fifty years from now."

Yes, he could sing as well as preach. At times he would suddenly sing during a sermon to illustrate a point, or he would leave the pulpit to play some chords on a piano or an organ. His versatility was amazing. He was a platform lecturer of the first rank. His knowledge of hymnology—both words and music—was encyclopædic. Not only did he largely shape the present "Methodist Hymn Book," but he went all over the country conducting choir rehearsals and otherwise introducing it to the people.

It was characteristic of this eager, untiring worker that he said some years ago: "I may be getting to the end of my career down here, but the Lord has given me a pretty good training as a quick-change artist, and I expect as soon as I go up there He will have some fresh job ready for me."

Dr. Wiseman had the humility which is one of the marks of true greatness. With all his gifts and all his fame, he was still quite unaffected, never presuming on the position to which he had attained, but always ready to serve his brethren and his Church even in obscure and untrodden ways.

The last time I heard Dr. Wiseman he was in his 84th year, but he was still impressive in his extraordinary vitality—physical and mental. There was always something dramatic about him—in his appearance, in his voice, in his whole bearing. But it all came to him quite naturally; there was never the least suggestion of any kind of posing. For a man of his years his voice was wonderful. After all the excessive demands he made upon it for so long a period, there were few signs of strain. It was still deep, striking, mellow, and he used it like a master as he had always done.

After the reading of the New Testament lesson (Mark, chapter 4) he said as he closed the Bible: "Thanks be unto God for His Gospel." It came unexpectedly in place of the usual phrase used by ministers.

Dr. Wiseman still believed in children's addresses, and we were all delighted when he said: "I want to tell the boys and girls a story of the last war." The story was that of a Commanding Officer's practice every morning. He said: "I bring myself to attention; make my salute to the Captain of my salvation, and say: 'What are my orders for to-day?'" Dr. Wiseman advised his hearers to begin every morning in the same way. "Pull yourself together in the presence of God; stand still and make your salute; get your orders before you go about your business for the day in the strength of Him who gives the orders. It won't take long, but it has wondrous effects."

We sang Godfrey Thring's hymn, "Fierce raged the tempest o'er the deep," and it was a fitting prelude to a sermon on Christ stilling the tempest, the text being His question: "Why are ye so fearful? How is it that ye have no faith?" There were vivid and arresting passages delivered with dramatic effect in describing the scene on the stormy sea. And there were oratorical passages possible only to a born orator like Dr. Wiseman. But what was most impressive of all was the revelation of sheer preaching power. There is a difference between sermon-making and preaching; this was preaching.

Dr. Wiseman had much to say about faith and he gave a definition of it which is worth quoting. In the storm at sea, faith was "confidence in Christ as able and willing to act suitably to the occasion." In his final passage he said the real question was: "Is Jesus in the boat?" Some nations had taken Him on board, but since have cast Him out. "My concern for this nation at this hour," he added, "is to make sure that Jesus is still in the boat."

Then he concluded with these words: "If I cannot tell you at what exact spot our boat may land, yet I know that on that spot on the other side which was in His mind we shall arrive." It was fitting that after that triumphant declaration the service should conclude with John Wesley's hymn, "Peace, doubting heart," with its closing lines:

> My soul a sudden call shall feel,
> And hear a whisper: Peace, be still!

Now the preacher's soul has felt that sudden call; his boat has landed; he has arrived on the other side.

> O then what raptured greetings
> On Canaan's happy shore.

January 22, 1944

LV

ARCHBISHOP TEMPLE

THE sudden death of Dr. William Temple, Archbishop of Canterbury, will be felt in Presbyterian Scotland as a personal loss. Although, unlike his predecessor, he was neither a Scotsman nor the son of a Presbyterian minister, he had many affinities with the Churches north of the Tweed, and he seemed to enjoy his frequent visits to Scotland.

Glasgow was the scene of one of his notable triumphs when he delivered his Gifford Lectures at the University on "Nature, Man, and God." These attracted such large audiences that the Humanity Class Room—usually large enough—was crowded out, and the lectures had to be transferred to the Upper Fore Hall.

Some of us also remember the wisdom, skill, and charm of personality with which he presided over the Faith and Order Conference at Edinburgh, winning the confidence and esteem of the representatives of many Churches on the occasion of that landmark in ecclesiastical history.

More than once he was a visitor to the General Assembly of the Church of Scotland. In the midst of a busy week of engagements he travelled north to Edinburgh to be present at the Assembly of 1939, when the Moderator was Professor Archibald Main, who had been a personal friend since the days when they were fellow-students in Balliol College, Oxford. He had a great welcome, and he gave the Assembly what was both an oration and a powerful and searching address.

It was characteristic of the Archbishop to keep his friendships in repair. The late Dr. G. C. Cossar of Glasgow, so well known as a social worker, as well as an earnest Evangelical, had been a class-fellow of William Temple at Rugby, where they shared a room. In later years they went their different ways and developed along different lines. But they kept up a continuous correspondence, and the Archbishop never came to Scotland without finding time amid the most important engagements to visit his old schoolmate and spend some time in his company.

The career of William Temple was in many ways an extraordinary one. There was a time when he was said to have been

ARCHBISHOP TEMPLE

To face page 188

regarded as being like Winston Churchill in the sense that anything might happen to him and everything might be possible for him. Then there came another period when, long before it came true, he seemed to be accepted as inevitably destined for the Primacy of All England.

Dr. Temple's massive figure has been the subject of many a facetious reference. "The square head very upright, the broad shoulders well back, the whole stocky figure like a rock confronts us," said one description, "with something of the challenge of the Sphinx." A certain Pickwickian aspect made him a gift to the cartoonist. The twinkle behind his spectacles was quite natural; he had a ready gift of humour; and all who knew him at close quarters were familiar with his loud infectious laugh, as boisterous as a schoolboy's. His personal habits were simple and almost austere. When he was translated from York to Canterbury he said: "My wife and I hope to create a small maisonette for ourselves inside the shell of Lambeth Palace." A non-smoker himself, he respected the habits of others. When presiding at an official dinner he would remark at the appropriate time with a disarming smile: "Gentlemen—if you must—you may smoke." One of his gifts was a happy knack of achieving popularity without courting it.

While some regretted his frank outspokenness on political and social questions, their criticisms never disturbed him. He went on his way just the same. And everyone had to admire the readiness with which he would face any type of audience in the most unorthodox surroundings, and not only talk freely but submit to heckling by his hearers. That was shown on a visit he paid to Clydebank when he addressed a great street-corner meeting of shipbuilding workers and gave ready answers to a rapid fire of questions.

Mr. David Williamson, in his volume on "Religion in the King's Reign," published in 1935, said: "The Church of England has in her Archbishops two powerful pulpit forces. Dr. Cosmo Gordon Lang is perhaps a more polished orator than Dr. William Temple. The latter inherited from his father, the late Archbishop Temple, a downright, outspoken manner which has endeared him to the men of the North of England. He argues a case with skill and tolerance, and never descends to the utterance of platitudes."

That was true then, and it remained true, and gave Dr. Temple his singular appeal to the common people. At the same time he could talk to philosophers and theologians in their own language and meet them on their own ground. Some would say he was a greater philosopher than a theologian and others that he was a greater theologian than a philosopher. Perhaps few men combined the two in such a marked degree.

It was characteristic of him that he said some time ago: "I am sure we must go to the people more than we have done, instead of expecting them to come to us. We need two things. We need supplementary forms of service for those who are not ready to participate in our accustomed forms of morning or evening prayer—not as substitutes for these but in addition to them. But we also need to make our traditional forms as valuable as possible to our people, always remembering the man or woman who may be in the church for the first time in many years."

Then he had a straight word to the clergy: "Above all, the actual conduct of the service needs constant vigilance lest we fall into some rut or habit which renders our reading of it lifeless. In some churches the prayers are gabbled. It is a standing temptation to the clergy to take the service in the way which is most expressive, and therefore most impressive to themselves. But this, in fact, is rank selfishness. Our task in public worship is to lead the worship of the people."

To the last Dr. Temple retained a certain youthfulness of spirit and this gained for him the ear of the rising generation. In a memorable address he declared that the two qualities which should be the contribution of young people to the life of the Church were loyalty and adventure. "The loyalty of Christian youth," he said, "must be first and foremost to Christ Himself. Nothing can take the place of the daily time of intimate companionship with the Lord. Make time for it, somehow and secure that it is real. This loyalty to Christ will find expression through active and eager membership of His Church. This again need not, and should not, imply a passive docility in place of the counsel of elders."

He continued: "We want people who are ready to make adventure. Some of the adventures will end in disappointment. Some of them will bring rebukes from ecclesiastical authorities, middle-aged folk like myself, who will be shocked and horrified. Never mind. Sometimes the adventurers will be right and the authorities wrong. But we need men who will seek the guidance of the Spirit of Christ to determine what is right and will give themselves to it heart and soul. Adventure and loyalty to Christ is what we want."

Never, perhaps, was the spirit of the man more clearly revealed than at his dedication as Archbishop of Canterbury, when he used words spoken by his father at his enthronement 45 years earlier. "I would rather," he said, "that my intimate friends knew me as one who thought nothing of himself in comparison with the work he had to do, rather than that they knew me as a great scholar or a great saint."

It was this spirit which gave him in his later days his almost unprecedented place in the confidence and esteem of the churches of all denominations. No one seemed more likely than he to exercise a profound and lasting influence on the religious and social life of our time and in the ecumenical movement which aims at the reunion of the Christian Churches. He will be mourned as a lost leader, and he will be sadly missed in the public arena. Yet many will rather cherish the memory of him as a simple, sincere soul, the man of great gifts who had no personal ends to serve, never presuming on his position, but glad to be the servant of all.

I heard many of Dr. Temple's great public orations both before and after he was Archbishop of Canterbury. It was impossible not to admit and admire the power and sweep of them. But he never appealed to me so much, or impressed me so deeply, as in the simple broadcast services he conducted from his own study at New Year time. Even across the wireless one caught something of the family atmosphere, and the Archbishop was so natural and homely and tender that his words must have appealed to hearers as those of a humble, sincere Christian speaking to his fellows as one of themselves and entirely forgetful of his high office.

And I shall always remember a young man telling of how he had been leaving the Royal Albert Hall, London, after a mass meeting which had been addressed by the Archbishop. He expected to see His Grace entering his car or calling a taxi, but instead he was queuing up to await a bus. The young man offered to hail a taxi for him, but the Archbishop courteously declined, saying he preferred to go by bus. Soon the two of them, the Primate of All England and the unknown young man, were in friendly and earnest conversation on the subject which had been under discussion at the meeting.

It was an incident that revealed something of the real greatness as well as the personal simplicity of William Temple, Archbishop of Canterbury, whose death is so deeply deplored to-day.

October 28, 1944

LVI

Dr. GEORGE JACKSON

IN his later years Dr. George Jackson was known chiefly as a writer, but it was as a preacher that he first achieved fame. The story of how he came north as a young minister to Edinburgh, and in that citadel of Presbyterianism and city of preachers made Methodism a living force in the community, while establishing himself as a leading pulpit figure, has in it an element of real romance.

He arrived in Edinburgh, a young man of 23, another "Little Minister" like J. M. Barrie's Gavin Dishart, and looking even less than his years. He had enthusiasm and he had ideas, but even in his dreams he had no vision of the great movement he was destined to inaugurate. All he set out to accomplish was "to do for the Methodists on the west side of the city what Nicolson Square Church was doing on the east side."

The first place of meeting he secured was a hall which he described as "a place of entertainment, not of the highest class, and in a general air of faded tawdriness." It was, however, on a main thoroughfare just beyond the west end of Princes Street, and 600 people could be crowded into it. In two years this hall was crowded out, and George Jackson made his first bold venture in leasing the United Presbyterian Synod Hall in Castle Terrace for his evening services.

This hall was then one of the largest in Edinburgh, with seating accommodation for about two thousand, and many regarded the young Methodist's move as a rather too daring experiment. His wisdom and foresight and faith were, however, soon justified. The Sunday evening services in the Synod Hall became one of the institutions of Edinburgh. Week after week the large building was crowded to overflowing, and this went on for some ten or eleven years with no sign of any falling off in the interest or the attendances. This was all the more noteworthy because of the fact that close at hand, in their historic pulpits, were two of the outstanding preachers of Edinburgh at that time—Dr. Alexander Whyte of St. George's and Dr. James Macgregor of St. Cuthbert's.

Eventually it came to be recognised that if the work of the

Principal
W. M. MACGREGOR

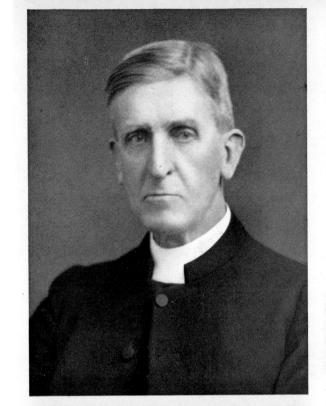

Dr.
G. H. MORRISON

Dr.
GEORGE JACKSON

Dr.
F. L. WISEMAN

West End Mission was to be stabilised, it must find a home of its own, and a central site was secured at Tollcross, where a splendid suite of buildings, erected at a cost of over £50,000, was opened with a memorable service, in which leading churchmen of various denominations, including Principal Rainy and Dr. Cameron Lees of St. Giles' Cathedral, took part. The Edinburgh Methodist Mission Hall is George Jackson's great memorial in the Scottish capital.

From the outset he had won the goodwill of the community by the clear statement he made as to the aim and purpose of his work. "We are not here," he said, "to make Presbyterians into Methodists. From the first day of our existence we have set our faces like a flint against proselytising in any form. Christ's army is none the stronger merely because a hundred of His soldiers are persuaded to change their regiments, though, of course, there may be individual cases in which the change is an advantage all round; and I often tell my people that, if ever the day should come (which God in His mercy forbid) when all that we can do is to lead saints to change their 'ism,' and not sinners to change their lives, they will need to look out for a new Superintendent."

Such a spirit engendered friendship, and he received encouragement and assistance from many of the most prominent Presbyterians. His work aroused in a special degree the admiration and sympathy of Dr. Alexander Whyte, who followed it with eager interest and ready help. Men as different from each other as Professor Marcus Dods and Dr. George Matheson, Dr. Walter C. Smith, Professor A. H. Charteris, and Dr. John Smith of Broughton Place, were among his other friends and helpers.

One special feature of George Jackson's preaching was the influence it exercised over young men, and notably over students preparing for the ministry. They flocked to his Synod Hall services in large numbers, and they were representative of many denominations. In his closing years, Dr. Jackson was an honoured visitor at the meetings of the General Assembly of the Church of Scotland, and it must have been one of the crowning joys of his life when ministers of that Church, including ex-Moderators, Professors and officials, were eager to recall his Sunday evenings in the Synod Hall, when they had sat at his feet and, through all the intervening years, had carried with them the influence of his preaching.

He brought something fresh and stimulating to the Edinburgh

13

pulpit in those days. It was not that there was anything even approaching sensationalism in his preaching, nor was there any oratorical display. His style was terse and incisive rather than rhetorical. Always he was supremely interesting and vivid. He could arrest attention and stimulate thought. That was part of the secret of his appeal to students and ministers, young and old. Never was there any display of fireworks, while his gestures, far from being dramatic, were almost unnoticeable. But it was essentially vital preaching. He himself once wrote: "There is passion in the rainbow-coloured reverie of Jeremy Taylor, and in the white art of John Henry Newman, in the raging, roaring flame of Whitefield, and in the still soundless heat of Wesley." And so, in Jackson's own preaching there was an underlying passion which every hearer felt, although there might be no sparks flying.

His sermons were often studded with literary quotations and allusions. I recall one service, long after his Edinburgh days, at which, in his illustrations, he drew on Tennyson's "The Lord of Burleigh," Charles Kingsley's "Alton Locke," Mark Rutherford's "Autobiography," "The Letters of James Smetham," George Eliot's "Romola," Robert Louis Stevenson, and a modern novelist. Yet one never felt it was overdone. Everything was used as an aid to exposition by a bookman who was drawing in the most natural way on his inexhaustible stores of literary knowledge.

For George Jackson was always a bookman, with an insatiable and an infectious interest in literature. It would be difficult to reckon all that he and W. J. Dawson and F. A. Atkins accomplished through the columns of the *Young Man* in encouraging a love of reading, and of the best reading, among the young men of those now distant days.

The same kind of influence he continued to exercise in the years of his prime, and even in his old age, through his "Free Church Notes" in the *Manchester Guardian*, and his weekly "Parson's Log" in the *Methodist Recorder*. In the latter, for many years, he proved the guide, philosopher, and friend of readers of all classes and of all denominations, ministers and laymen alike, reaching more people outside Methodism than perhaps the Methodists ever fully realised. He had the gifts of the real essayist and could give interest and charm to any subject. But ever and anon he was back among the books he loved and taught others to love. On him in a very special measure there seemed to have fallen the mantle of Robertson Nicoll as a writer on books and bookmen.

Preaching was another great theme to which he returned again and again in his press articles.   One series may be recalled in which he dealt with such aspects as, "Is Preaching Worth While?" "Is Modern Preaching Too Quiet?" "Impersonal Preaching," "Painful Preaching," "The Pulpit Scold," "Concerning Jargon," "Speech Easy to be Understood," and "The Taking Gift of Unction."   Fortunately, like many of his other writings, these have been included in his published works which extend altogether to nearly twenty volumes, and will keep his name alive for years to come.

In all his preaching and in all his writing George Jackson never lost hold of the essentials.   There had been times when some of his more conservative colleagues considered him somewhat advanced.   But with all his modern outlook, he was always true to the verities of the faith, and behind his culture there was felt the throbbing of a heart in tune with the infinite.   His own faith was a radiant one as he once proclaimed it in a characteristic passage: "We are not orphans in a cold world, unshepherded and uncared for:

> Poor Windlestraws,
> On the great, sullen, roaring pool of Time,
> And Chance and Change . . .

We are in the hands of God."   His preaching had the true Evangelical note, and also what a writer long ago described as that indefinable spiritual particle which links George Jackson to John Wesley.

Personally George Jackson was one of the most modest of men. With all his shining gifts he remained utterly unassuming.   He was of a companionable nature, making friends and grappling them to his soul with hooks of steel.   His memory will live in the hearts of those who loved him for what he was, and who loved him the better the longer they knew him.

April 21, 1945

LVII

Dr. G. CAMPBELL MORGAN

IN Dr. Campbell Morgan the Methodists lost one of the great preachers of his time, but their loss was the gain of the Congregationalists. In a sense he became the property of all the Churches, for he was too big a figure to be affected by the usual denominational distinctions. But it is strange now to recall the circumstances which led to his change-over in the early days of his career.

He had begun to preach while he was still in his teens, but stress of family circumstances made it necessary for him to accept an appointment as a day-school teacher. Even then he went on preaching because of an inward urge that could not be ignored, and eventually he applied for admission to the ministry of the Methodist Church in which he had been brought up and in connection with which he had been serving as an evangelist.

In that year one hundred and fifty candidates offered themselves for the ministry, and out of this number one hundred and five were rejected, Campbell Morgan being one of them. Great preacher as he afterwards became, he failed in his "trial" sermon. His ordeal was in a church seated for a thousand people and only seventy-five were in the pews. His courage failed him, and he did not pass the test of his examiners. It may be idle to conjecture as to what extent he was affected by the atmosphere. But in his later life he was always susceptible to his environment. After he had become famous he once remarked, "Always, I would rather address a thousand people than one. For me an ideal existence would be a house buried in the woods, a quiet transit to a crowded church, and—back again to the woods!"

Undaunted, and still without any training in a Divinity Hall, he went on preaching, and in his many missions he attracted and impressed masses of people all over England. Then he was called to a Congregational church in a small town in North Staffordshire, where he was ordained in 1889. After two busy happy years he was afterwards at Rugeley before he went to his first important charge in Birmingham—a Congregational church to which he had been very strongly recommended by one of his Methodist "trial judges" who had "failed" him for the Methodist ministry.

From Birmingham he went to London, with the church life of which his name was to be so prominently identified over a long stretch of years.

The success of his ministry in the historic New Court Congregational Church became one of the features of the religious life of London, but within four years he was off to America, to which his fame had also spread. In this and some other stages in his career restlessness was said to be his besetting sin. For three years he served as Northfield Conference Extension Lecturer, travelling all over the United States and also sharing in the Northfield Conferences inaugurated by D. L. Moody. Then came the call to return to London to be minister of Westminster Chapel, and he entered on his first term of service there. It lasted for fifteen years, until once more he decided to return to America, where he carried on preaching and lecturing work on independent lines. Last of all came his return to Westminster Chapel, London, which was to be the scene of the remaining years of his active ministry. Incidentally he acted for a short time also as President of Cheshunt College, Cambridge, but in that academic appointment he was not in his element.

Dr. Campbell Morgan was first and always a preacher. When it was once said to him, "You can preach and you know it," he frankly replied, "I have no hesitation in affirming I *can* preach. I do not know anything else under the sun of which I am willing to make a similar affirmation. I am sure I dare not say I can sing, and no friend of mine would suspect me of saying I can play golf. I can preach. It is the one thing I want to do and cannot help doing. I would do it as a recreation if I was not permitted to do it as a vocation."

This passion for preaching was one of the secrets of his success. He owed little if anything to that personal fascination which often counts for so much. His appearance in the pulpit was impressive and arresting rather than attractive. "As one saw him in profile," said a graphic description, "he appeared to be little more than a loose-jointed framework, upon which were hung his garments of ample broadcloth. This framework was turreted by a great head, mostly nose and mouth, and flowing locks. The cords of his long neck appeared to be striving to separate themselves from his flesh."

In the pulpit Campbell Morgan's tall, gaunt figure seemed to move somewhat stiffly and awkwardly at first, but once he had plunged into his subject there was a wonderful transformation.

The whole man appeared to palpitate with an uncontrollable energy; he preached with every fibre of his being. You could see how he was dominated himself—and the preacher who is gripped by his own message does not fail to grip his hearers. He cultivated neither daintiness of style nor sensationalism of speech, neither a wealth of paradox nor a display of phrasecraft. He fed his hearers on strong meat, and gave them quantity as well as quality. Every discourse was something of a theological treatise, but always with a very definite and practical application.

When he was once asked how he made his sermons he said: "I can only give you some very general statements as to my methods. Two things are vital: first, personal first-hand work on the text; and then, all scholarly aids obtainable. I never take down a commentary until I have done personal, first-hand work, and have made my outline. Sometimes after consulting scholarly aids I have to alter the outline; but at anyrate I have had the benefit of first-hand work. We make a mistake when we have a text that has gripped us, or better, has found us; and turn to commentaries first. To do that is to create a second-hand mentality. The first thing is to work on the text itself."

A final word of advice he gave to preachers was: "There is a sense in which preaching is a conflict, a conflict with your hearers. I do not like the word conflict, but I do not know a better. The preacher is not merely asking a congregation to discuss a situation, and consider a proposition, or give attention to a theory. We are out to storm the citadel of the will, and capture it for Jesus Christ. Whether evangelizing or teaching does not matter. The appeal is the final thing. I have always felt, and never more so than now, that the work of preaching is not that of debating difficulties, or speculating, or considering philosophies, but that of proclaiming the Word of God."

The late Frederick A. Atkins once said: "It is an astonishing revelation that the man who can gather congregations as large if not larger than any other preacher in Britain, the United States, or Canada, invariably offers those congregations by way of a sermon fifty minutes to an hour of close-fitting elaborate argument. Dr. Morgan has never belonged to the 'short and snappy' school of preachers. He will not attempt to overpower you with rhetoric, or entertain you with ancient anecdotes, or surprise you with dexterous illustrations, or dazzle you with brilliant quotations. Not at all. But he will—for nearly an hour—build up a solid, sustained, carefully thought-out and apparently unanswerable

DR. G. CAMPBELL MORGAN

argument, which you would not expect to be irresistibly attractive. Still, people crowd to hear it, from Los Angeles to London. from the sunny Gulf of Mexico to the muddy Mersey. Wherever he goes people quickly discover him or hasten to renew acquaintance with him, and crowd to listen to him, although he does little except to expound a Book which clever critics tell us is no longer read!"

From first to last Campbell Morgan was a Biblical preacher. His aim was that of an expositor, and he consistently maintained a teaching ministry. In both terms at Westminster Chapel he attracted crowds not only to his Sunday services, but also to his week-night Bible School which was for years something unique in the life of London, attracting students of all ages and from all churches and denominations.

His teaching ministry was not confined to his pulpit or his Bible School. It was also exercised through his numerous published works. These have attained large circulations all over the English-speaking world, attracting Fundamentalist and Modernist readers alike in a way few theological works have done. This wider teaching ministry of his fortunately continues although his voice is now silent. His books are still being read and consulted, and are likely to be so for years to come, while new ones unpublished at the time of his death are coming from the press.

Campbell Morgan was an aristocrat of the pulpit with the command of a perfect artistry. His voice had qualities all its own; his elocution was perfect, and his dramatic power was of no mean order. He was a master of the grand manner of pulpit oratory. But, before all and above all, he was a "Preacher of the Word." That had been his aim throughout all his life and he pursued it with an undeviating purpose.

It would be difficult to assess the supreme value of his work in helping to rediscover the English Bible to multitudes of men and women.

June 2, 1945

ALPHABETICAL INDEX

	PAGE		PAGE
BOOTH, General William	53	McINTOSH, Rev. Donald	98
CAIRNS, Principal John	57	McINTYRE, Dr. D. M.	128
CHALMERS, James	35	MACKINTOSH, Professor H. R.	148
CONNOR, Ralph	92	McNEILL, Rev. John	31
DAWSON, Rev. W. J.	75	MATHESON, Dr. George	14
DENNEY, Principal James	161	MEYER, Dr. F. B.	134
DODS, Dr. Marcus	142	MOFFATT, Professor James	89
FAIRBAIRN, Principal A. M.	27	MORGAN, Dr. G. Campbell	196
FINDLAY, Pastor D. J.	151	MORISON, Principal James	64
FLEMING, Dr. Archibald	155	MORRISON, Dr. George H.	179
FRASER, Dr. Donald	101	MORTON, Professor Robert	110
GLADSTONE, Rev. George	158	PARKER, Dr. Joseph	39
GRIEVE, Dr. Alexander	122	PATON, John G.	35
HASTINGS, Dr. James	113	PATERSON, Professor W. P.	131
HORNE, Rev. C. Silvester	68	SHEPHERD, Dr. Ambrose	85
HORTON, Dr. R. F.	116	SMELLIE, Dr. Alexander	95
HUGHES, Rev. Hugh Price	82	SMITH, Professor David	19
HUNTER, Dr. John	50	SMITH, Dr. Walter C.	104
JACKSON, Dr. George	192	STALKER, Professor James	42
JONES, Dr. J. D.	167	STODDART, Rev. William	140
JOWETT, Dr. J. H.	60	STRUTHERS, Rev. J. P.	164
KELMAN, Dr. John	124	TALMAGE, Dr. T. De Witt	71
KENNEDY, Rev. G. A. Studdert	137	TATTERSALL, Rev. T. N.	170
KER, Dr. John	107	TEMPLE, Archbishop	188
LAWS, Dr. Robert	46	WATSON, Dr. John	176
LAX, Rev. W. H.	173	WHITHAM, Rev. A. E.	119
MACDONALD, Dr. George	79	WHYTE, Dr. Alexander	11
MACGREGOR, Dr. James	24	WISEMAN, Dr. F. L.	185
MACGREGOR, Principal W. M.	182	YOUNG, Dr. Dinsdale T.	145